ON THE ROAD WITH BILL CLINTON

MAX MARKSON

Published by:
Wilkinson Publishing Pty Ltd
ACN 006 042 173
Level 4, 2 Collins Street
Melbourne, Vic 3000
Ph: 03 9654 5446
www.wilkinsonpublishing.com.au

Copyright © 2018 Max Markson

All rights reserved. No part of this publication may be reproduced, stored in a retrieval system or transmitted in any form by any means without the prior permission of the copyright owner. Enquiries should be made to the publisher.

Every effort has been made to ensure that this book is free from error or omissions. However, the Publisher, the Author, the Editor or their respective employees or agents, shall not accept responsibility for injury, loss or damage occasioned to any person acting or refraining from action as a result of material in this book whether or not such injury, loss or damage is in any way due to any negligent act or omission, breach of duty or default on the part of the Publisher, the Author, the Editor, or their respective employees or agents.

A catalogue record for this book is available from the National Library of Australia

Planned date of publication: 10-2018
Title: On the Road with Bill Clinton
ISBN(s): 9781925642490 : Printed - Paperback

Design by Spike Creative Pty Ltd
Ph: (03) 9427 9500
spikecreative.com.au

Printed in Australia by Griffin Press

Text font is Janson Text 11/16pt

To my beautiful wife Kanchi,
You are the love of my life and my soul enchantress.

CONTENTS

Introduction 7

1. The Full Nelson Experience
   Nelson Mandela (2000) 13

2. Dollar Bill
   Bill Clinton (2001-06) 27

3. On the Road with Bill Clinton 47

4. The President, the Vice President and Fat Tony
   George Bush Snr and Al Gore (2001, 2007) 61

5. Mr New York City
   Rudy Giuliani (2003) 73

6. Keeping Up with the Kardashians
   Kim Kardashian (2010) 87

7. The Blair Rich Project
   Tony Blair (2011) 103

8. I like Mike
   Mike Tyson (2012) 115

9. Hasta la vista, Arnie
   Arnold Schwarzenegger (2013-18) 129

10. Gooooaaaallll
    Pele (2015) 145

11. Raquel, Rachel and Pamela (2000-2013) 157

INTRODUCTION

I'm a name-dropper. I admit it. In my line of work you have to be. The names of the people you have worked with successfully in the past are your calling card, your introduction, your CV, all in two words — or in the case of Pele, one word.

Those of you who read my first book, *Show Me the Money*, will know that I am a showman's son from Bournemouth in England who came out to Australia about 40 years ago with a few quid in my pocket and a big smile on my face, and made good. After learning the business as a promotions manager for various local businesses and a radio station, in 1982 I went out on my own and opened my PR agency, Markson Sparks!

I wouldn't say we were an overnight success, it probably took a couple of months, but with a bit of luck, an awful lot of hard work and even more of what I call chutzpah, pretty soon Markson Sparks! was one of the busiest — and certainly the best known — promotion companies in the country.

As I wrote in *Show Me the Money*, 'We specialise in PR, promotions, personal management, fundraising, corporate functions and elephant races. Of course, a lot of people specialise in PR, promotions, personal management, fundraising and corporate functions. It's the elephant races that have set me apart from the rest.'

I don't organise too many elephant races these days, although if someone asked me to I would, and while a big part of my business remains PR, promotions and personal representation, I now have a new specialisation which has seen me rub shoulders with some of the biggest names in the world.

To all those other services I have added to my business card 'International Celebrity Speaking Agency'.

Show Me the Money came out in early 2000 which was a big year for me — and the country. The Olympics were held in Sydney, and I had a voluntary gig when I was appointed assistant media director for the Australian Olympic team. I got a uniform and everything, but that was just the half of it. Around the same time (exactly the same time in fact) I was given the opportunity to organise a series of functions in Sydney for arguably the best known and most respected person on the planet, Nelson Mandela. It was my first experience of dealing with a really big-name international personality, but if you're going to try something new, why not start at the top?

As I said earlier, the name Nelson Mandela is a good one to drop when you are trying to work with other international figures of note. It certainly didn't hurt when I was negotiating with Bill Clinton's people 12 months later to say that I had dealt successfully with Mandela and raised the best part of $1 million for his charity. Likewise, when I could tell the representatives of President George Bush Snr and Mayor Rudy Giuliani that I had delivered for President Clinton on the first of what would eventually be four speaking tours, it was a major factor in them agreeing to me hosting their visits in 2001 and 2003.

On and on it went, one name-drop leading to the next, but that is not what this book is about. If names are all you are after, just look at the table of contents. What I am doing here is telling the stories behind the names, letting you share in the privileged world that I have been privy to for almost 20 years.

That is honestly how I look at it: a privilege. There have been times when I have been rubbing shoulders with world leaders in the most relaxed environment and felt like pinching myself. I've sat on a boat eating sweets and singing songs with Bill Clinton and shared breakfast in Rudy Giuliani's hotel suite as the sun came up in Perth. I've thought to myself, 300 million people in the US can't get near these men, and yet here I am, a kid from Bournemouth sharing a block of chocolate with one or asking another to pass the salt.

Sure, there is a work element to it, and it's hard work too. Try organising a 500-seat $10,000 a table function on a month's notice, or carrying a heavy media wall around the US and Canada and setting it up night after night as the backdrop for a Kim Kardashian appearance. Better still, try getting a good night's sleep when you've just guaranteed to pay over $2 million to a former world leader knowing you haven't got that sort of money in the bank.

Not that I am complaining in any way, shape or form. I'm just saying that while dealing with some of the world's best-known celebrities is work, to me it is much, much more than that. I'm not just interested in the bottom line, I'm interested in the people themselves and cannot believe that

I am in a position to not just meet them, but to spend time with them and get to know them.

Time is the key word. With some of the big names I have worked with my interaction is little more than a quick meeting, a handshake and the opportunity to watch how they work and interact with others. They arrive, they do a function or two and head straight back to the airport. With others, though, the visits are longer, my involvement more hands-on, and the chance for us to get to know each other far greater.

Breaking the ice with these people, as with anyone you meet, is not an instantaneous process, but it is a process I love. Our first meeting is usually rather formal, as you can imagine when you are discussing large sums of money, but once the deal making is out of the way and the tour has commenced things warm up. We're pretty much hanging out with each other for days, sometimes weeks at a time, in planes, at hotels and functions.

I'm always on my best behaviour at first, but as soon as the mood relaxes I start enjoying myself, and making sure my new friends do too. As anyone who knows me knows only too well, I'm a different sort of character. Maybe it's from growing up around the Leon Markson Aquashow where I made my theatrical debut as a fish with a torch in my mouth, floating around on my back during the grand finale. Unfortunately, that was the highlight of my stage career but the performing bug is never far from the surface, so to speak. Given half a chance — or even less than half — I like to tell a corny joke, make some ridiculous pun or break out into song. That's just who I am and I will always be myself, no matter whether I'm with the man behind the counter in the grocery store or the former President of the United States of America.

Funny thing is, the former President seems to enjoy it more than the grocer. I think maybe that's because when you are the most powerful man in the world you're not used to people treating you as if you are a real person. People like Bill Clinton or Rudy Giuliani are not used to someone letting their guard down in front of them and that means they can't let down their guard either.

With me, they can be themselves, and that's why I have got along so well with many of them. Some I consider friends, and believe they feel the same about me. I have been myself, and so have they. What do we talk about in those private times? Anything and everything. I tell them my life story, they tell me theirs. They tell me about their ambitions and what they hope to achieve now that they are out of public office. Hopefully, through my fundraising expertise I'm able to help them realise those ambitions.

Most of all, I get to know them. The real them.

Whenever I have just finished a tour with a celebrity the first thing I am asked is, 'what were they really like?'

Read on and you will find out.

CHAPTER I
THE FULL NELSON EXPERIENCE
NELSON MANDELA (2000)

I'm putting Nelson Mandela at the start of this book for three reasons: One, along with President Clinton, he's the biggest name I have ever worked with; two, he taught me an awful lot, and three, he was the first big international 'star' I promoted in Australia. As I see it, if you're going to make a list, doing it chronologically is as good a way as any.

President Mandela first came into my life, so to speak, in 2000. It was, as is so often the case in my line of work, something of a happy accident. Something you do for a few dollars and a bit of fun leads to something else, which leads to something else. Most of all, it leads to creating friendships and contacts, and in the world of the 'Three P's' — public relations, publicity and promotion — contacts are everything.

Back in the late 1990s, I was approached by a guy named Richard Lubner to promote his One World Sports Bar at Darling Harbour in Sydney. Richard was a former professional tennis player from South Africa who took a gamble on the fact that Australians would want to sit around and drink beer while watching sport on giant TV screens. Needless to say, the gamble paid off, but in the early days he needed some help getting the word out. I've always been a big believer that the best way to get publicity is to use celebrities and if you want to promote a sports bar, the celebrities you need are obviously sporting celebrities. We came up with an idea we called 'Sports Stars Behind The Bar'. It wasn't rocket science but it took off like Apollo 11. Basically, every Friday we'd have a few sports stars spend an hour or so serving behind the bar. We had top Test cricketers, big name rugby league and Sydney Swans players, and to add some beauty to the beasts, *Inside Sport* magazine put us in touch with their most popular cover girls. For $200 cash we'd have young models just making a name for themselves, like Annalise Braakensiek and Jodie Meares, working alongside the likes of Allan Border, Shane Warne and Jeff Fenech. Channel 10 used to do a live cross to their *Sports Tonight* show, the place was packed every Friday and we'd all go out to supper afterwards.

At the time it was a few dollars in the bank and a lot of fun, but if someone had said it would lead to me organising lunch with Nelson Mandela, I would have said they were nuts.

Even so, one day I received a call from Richard. I thought it was just a regular catch-up to check who we had lined up for the next Friday, but he shocked me.

'Hey Max,' he says. 'Do you want to bring Nelson Mandela to Australia?'

'Sure, but do you think he'll want to serve behind the bar?'

Richard told me that his father, back in South Africa, was a friend of Mandela's through his youth charity Tikun and if I was interested he could put in an offer to bring him out for some speaking engagements.

I did some sums and put an offer to him through Richard's father of $1 million. I didn't have a million dollars but I thought if we could get Nelson Mandela we'd make enough money to pay him.

The way it works with celebrities of that stature is that you offer them a set fee for a certain number of appearances. You then organise the events — usually for charity — charge admission, deduct your costs and fee and send a big cheque to the worthy cause of choice.

I sent off the offer to Richard's father in February 2000 and waited with interest for a reply. And waited and waited and waited. Then, in about the third week of July I'm reading the newspaper and see a story saying Mandela has announced he's coming to Australia in September. He is speaking at Sydney University and doing an enormous event in Melbourne with Reuben 'Hurricane' Carter on the bill.

I ring Richard and say, 'What's going on? I've offered $1 million, haven't heard back and now I read that he's coming'.

He says he doesn't know, but he'll find out. He comes back to me a few days later, says he's spoken to his dad who's spoken to Mandela who has apologised. He told Richard's father that his office had done all the arrangements, he didn't know the details, but he was happy to do the gigs for me for free.

Normally this would make me very happy. When it comes to negotiating with a celebrity for their services, 'free' is my favourite price but on this occasion there was a snag. A big one. About as big as you can get. The Sydney Olympics.

We are now at the end of July. Richard tells me Mandela is coming to Sydney on 3 September and I can do whatever I want to do on 4 September. Trouble is, the Olympics start on 15 September and in one of the highlights my career, I've have been appointed assistant media director of the Australian team. For weeks before the horses were due to come galloping out at the Opening Ceremony I would be working my tail off, dealing with the press, driving to and from the airport collecting dignitaries and hosing down pre-Games firestorms like blow-ups in the Aussie boxing team. Most of all, I'm due to check into the Olympic Village on 2 September — the day before Mandela arrives.

'It's too short notice,' I tell Richard. 'I'm not going to do it.'

He can't believe what he's hearing.

'It's Nelson Mandela,' he says.

I say I know, but it's a month to go. I haven't got time to do it. I've got other things on; I've got to get all my work done before I go into the village for a month.

He's begging now. 'You have to do it, it's Nelson Mandela'. I say leave it with me, I'll think about it overnight. Next day I tell him, 'oh all right then, I'll host Nelson Mandela'.

I decided to do a major public function on the Monday night, 4 September, and a private lunch earlier in the day. As we weren't paying Mandela a fee, all proceeds from the lunch would go straight to his charity. The money raised at the larger night function would be split between a number of local charities.

We set about organising the lunch function first, and

this is where Mandela, indirectly, opened my eyes to something I have seen many times since: the generosity of the very wealthy.

One doesn't have to look far to see the regard many people in the community have for the rich and famous. Social media and the online 'comments' sections of news websites provide a forum for their opinions, and they don't hold back. Invariably a news story about a well-known figure will bring forth a torrent of bitterness about the ill-deserved money they believe is being hoarded or squandered.

My experience has been very different, and the Mandela luncheon was the perfect example.

Given the limited time frame and my heavy commitments I came up with the idea of holding a private lunch for 20 people at $25,000 a head, earning Mandela's charity a quick half a million dollars. Sound simple? Well, surprisingly it was, thanks to a contact I made back in those days of 'Sports Stars Behind The Bar'. Remember Jodie Meares? Well, by this time she is no longer Jodie, she's Jodhi, and her surname isn't Meares, it's Packer. Through her flourishing swimwear company, Tiger Lilly, I reach out to Jodhi and ask her if she'll have a quiet word in the ear of her husband James Packer, which she kindly does and within a day or two I'm sitting in James's office in Park St.

I've known James for 12 years because he used to be best mates with Jeff Fenech whom I managed and from time to time he would come along to my functions. I explain to him my idea about the luncheon and ask him if he'll host it. He says, 'yeah I'll do it', and immediately buys five tickets for himself, his father Kerry, his lifelong mate and future Channel 9 boss David Gyngell, his financial advisor Ashok Jacob and Jeremy Phillips who is running the Packer's internet interests. So that's $125,000 and James's name on the invitations. Not a bad start. I come up with a list of 15 other people who I think would be good to invite. James drops a couple, adds a couple and my office sends out the invitations: Come to lunch with Nelson Mandela, James Packer is hosting, $25,000 a head. Most said yes, but it they said no, I'd report it back to James's office and within half an hour they'd say yes because James would say, 'you've got to come' and when a Packer says you've got to do something, you usually do.

In the end it was an impressive list of people and an amazing day. We held it at the Hilton Hotel where President Mandela was staying. They gave us a private dining room and we had done it up beautifully with a magnificent table setting by a guy named Phillip Carr who'd just arrived from South Africa six weeks before. He wanted some work from us. I asked him about his career highlights and he told me he'd done a function for Nelson Mandela. I said, 'Phillip, have I got a job for you...'

It was one big square table, with Mandela sitting between James and Kerry and the others seated around them. I didn't sit at the table. I rarely do at my own functions, unless there is a spare chair, as there was at an anniversary dinner I organised for Bob Hawke in 2003.

It was a fundraiser I put on to mark the 20th anniversary of Bob becoming prime minister, with the proceeds going to the Labor party and also his foundation. There was a spare seat between him and Solomon Lew so he said, 'Max sit here'. I said, 'yes sir', so I'm sitting between the former prime minister and one of the richest men in Australia as a table filler.

When the auction came on we auctioned a signed Rolling Stones guitar — one of 74 signed Rolling Stones guitars we've auctioned off — and I said to Solly, 'this would be a really good gift to give someone'. He said, 'Okay, I'll nudge you every time I want you to bid'. So he's digging me in the ribs and I'm sticking my hand up every time. You've no idea how much fun it can be spending someone else's money. I — well, Solly actually — bought it for $10,000 and gave it to investment guru Gary Weiss as a present.

There were no spare seats at James Packer's lunch for Mandela, and no auction either (I'd hate to think what would have happened if that room had got into a bidding war over a guitar), so I just stood to the side and watched and listened.

Mandela stood at a lectern and talked about South Africa, Australia, the world and charity and then each of the guests asked a question. I'd like to say I remember what each of them asked and what Mandela answered but I'm afraid the only thing that I can recall is that John Singleton asked him a question about boxing. From that you can gather that it was quite an informal occasion.

I have a photo of Mandela with James and his 18 guests. There was Singo, State Bank founder Robert Whyte, who was on the Packer's board, and corporate advisor David

Gonski. Packaging billionaire Richard Pratt couldn't come but he sent his son-in-law Raphael 'Ruffy' Geminder. There were also a couple of guys I'm guessing that James now wishes he hadn't invited — Brad Keeling and Jodee Rich, who started the phone company One.Tel, in which James and Lachlan Murdoch invested and lost an estimated $1 billion.

Oh, and two others. A 16-year-old boy, and a dork in an Olympic blazer.

The dork in the Olympic blazer, needless to say, was me. I had just moved into the Olympic village and had to get permission from Australian Olympic boss John Coates to leave the village on the Monday to attend the function. I told him I had to have lunch with Nelson Mandela. What was he going to say, 'no'? I suppose I could have worn a standard blue suit but hey, how many times do you get to walk around town in an Olympic uniform? So I wore my blazer, tie, the whole bit. I remember before Nelson arrived I'm standing with Singo and Kerry Packer having a chat — as much as you can have a chat with those two. If it's not about them, it's not of interest, but suddenly Kerry noticed my uniform.

'What are you supposed to be?' he said. I told him I was part of the Olympic team and that I was living at the Village. Suddenly I had his attention. He wanted all the gossip about who was hooking up with whom. I'm afraid I had to disappoint him.

'I've only been there two days,' I said, and he went back to Singo.

The 16-year-old was a schoolkid named Elliot Placks. A few weeks before the lunch he'd rung up and said, 'My Dad knows you. Can I come and do work experience at your place?' I said, 'sure, and wear a suit and tie just in case. You never know what might happen.'

As it happened his first day was that Monday, 4 September, so the kid comes along to the luncheon. When James goes up to get Mandela and bring him down I'm standing there with him at the side of the room. The doors open and in comes James and Mandela with a couple of security, and before James can start introducing Mandela to any of his guests he walks away from him, comes up to the kid, puts his arm around him and says, 'why aren't you at school today?'

Elliot is a real estate agent these days. I see him around sometimes and he always mentions that day. As you would. A 16-year-old meeting Nelson Mandela — it's not something you'd forget.

At the end of the day we were able to hand Mandela a cheque for $500,000 for his Mandela Children's Fund and Foundation. I was later told that between courses he had also put the hard word on Kerry for another million dollars for his charity. I'm not sure whether he got it, but you can't blame a former world leader for trying.

That evening we did a function in the ballroom for about 500 people, which, with only four and half weeks to pull it together gives an indication of Mandela's pulling power. The beverage and dairy giant Lion Nathan agreed to put in $200,000 as the naming rights sponsor, with one condition

— that I wasn't to be seen to have anything to do with it. I asked them why and they said it was because I was a 'brand'. Now I can see it, but back then I didn't see myself that way. To my mind I was just a PR man doing some events and promotions, but for $200,000 I was more than happy to take a back seat. I designed the invitations with a picture of Mandela and sold tickets, and they sold tickets. It sold out at $250 a head ($2,500 a table of ten) or $1,000 a head ($10,000 a VIP table of ten) for a VIP reception beforehand. These days my VIP tickets include a photo with the guest of honour but we couldn't do that with Mandela because his eyes couldn't take the flash.

It was an excellent function. I had invited, as my guests, people like former prime ministers Gough Whitlam, Bob Hawke and Malcolm Fraser, and the NSW Premier Bob Carr and they all came. I was chatting that night with Gough Whitlam and Bob Hawke when Gough says 'Is there any function or anything that happens in this town that you don't organise?' Everyone wanted to see and hear Nelson Mandela. He had an aura about him and on that visit he showed what made him such a respected and effective leader. He could be warm and funny, but also tough.

I got to see all those sides of him in a very short period of time.

After the private luncheon he was very happy with how everything had gone and pleased with the money we had raised for his function. I was running through the details for that night's function and he asked about the money being raised. When I told him that it would be split amongst a number of local charities he said he needed to speak to the Lion Nathan people. I arranged the meeting and, while I wasn't there, I was told they had a serious discussion in which he said he was going to pull out unless he got half the money for his charities in South Africa. With 500 people having already paid — and some already starting to arrive — they obviously agreed.

That was the tough side of Mandela — and there was more of that to come. The warm side was when the function was just getting underway. We had the Qantas youth choir singing the national anthem. When they were finished, Mandela got up from his seat, walked across and shook their hands and said 'thank you very much' to every single kid. I've never seen that before or since.

And the humorous side? When Mandela got up to speak he told the crowd, 'Normally when I come to these functions I only talk for 10 minutes or so and then I leave, but you are so important I will speak longer tonight.' Okay, so he wasn't Bob Hope, but the crowd loved it.

We weren't allowed to do a live auction but we did a silent auction that raised around $500,000. The prize item was one of Mandela's colourful shirts which he signed. I didn't have time to have it mounted and framed but it didn't matter. It went for $20,000. Seeing big dollars for my charity events I asked if he had any more, but I was told that it was his only spare. The others he had brought were for wearing. Pity, I could have raised a fortune. He did sign 15 books for me though and they proved to be the gift that kept on giving. The following year when I brought

President Clinton out to Australia I asked him to sign some books for me to be auctioned off. His minders told me that wouldn't be permitted. I said, 'but Nelson Mandela signed books for me' and they said, 'really? Okay then'.

The night was a huge success. Everyone loved Mandela, he seemed to be enjoying himself, and we cleared $500,000, half going back to South Africa and the rest split between the Children's Hospital at Westmead, Rev. Bill Crews' Exodus Foundation and Mission Australia.

Under the terms of our agreement those were the only two functions that Mandela and I were obligated to do together, but he had another meeting that he wanted me to organise — with the leaders of Sydney's Jewish community.

No problem. I rang around and got together all the top rabbis and heads of all the charities, about 50 or 60 in total, and they met at the Hilton the next night for a one hour meet and greet. As this wasn't a fundraiser and all I had done was send out some invitations, I didn't attend. It was just a room of gentlemen meeting up for a friendly chat. What could possibly go wrong?

Apparently, plenty. I was told that Mandela entered the room at 5pm on the dot and said hello. The Jewish leaders said hello back, and then they had a stand-up argument for an hour. He was berating them about how the Israelis were treating the Palestinians at the time and they were giving it back to him. It was obviously an issue he felt very strongly about and he wasn't going to miss an opportunity to let the leaders of Sydney's Jewish community know where he stood. I'm not sure if he held a similar meeting in Melbourne, or indeed everywhere else he travelled, but he certainly made his feelings known that night — as did his guests. At 6pm on the dot he said goodbye and left the room after what could be termed 'spirited discussion'.

My final encounter with Mandela was the next day when he visited the Olympic Athletes' Village. He met with the South African athletes and then did a short walk through, drawing an enormous crowd of admirers. I stood back and watched with some of the other Australian team officials. Not being from a sporting or even mainstream media background I was a bit of an outsider at that stage. No one really knew who I was or what to make of me, but Mandela was about to change that. As he was being escorted to his car he spotted me through the crowd and waved.

'Hello Max,' he said.

'Nelson,' I replied, as if this sort of thing happened to me every day.

In truth I never really got close to Mandela in a personal sense. We had no one-on-one time because his visit was really a hit-and-run operation piggy-backed onto the other events he was doing. Apart from the three functions I organised in two days, I had nothing to do with his itinerary or movements.

I was working at the Olympics and he was in the hands of the people who had brought him to Australia. Even so, I couldn't help but be impressed with his presence, his ability to work a crowd and his steely determination when it came to something he believed in.

I became a lifelong admirer — so much so that I have a

beautiful framed photo-portrait of him above my desk. We worked well together, we made some money for good causes and he opened many doors for me.

I couldn't say we became friends, but Bill Clinton? That's another story.

CHAPTER 2
DOLLAR BILL
BILL CLINTON (2001-06)

In early 2000 my first book *Show Me the Money* was released and one of the interviews I did as part of the promotional campaign was with *The Sydney Morning Herald*. The reporter asked, 'If there was one person — anyone in the world — that you could represent right now, who would it be?' I didn't hesitate. 'President Bill Clinton,' I said. It might seem an obvious answer now, but back then, not so much. For starters, President Clinton was still in office and he had a bit on his plate. Also, I wasn't in the international celebrity business at the time. My experience hosting Nelson Mandela in Sydney was still a few months off and I had no real idea of whether I would be capable of putting together a full tour with a person of that stature, or whether it would even be successful. I did have enormous respect for President Clinton however and I just had a hunch that given the chance, we could work well together. As it turned out, I wouldn't have to wait long to see if I was right.

President Clinton left office in January 2001 and I immediately started trying to bring him to Australia. As you can imagine, when opening negotiations with the former leader of the free world it's not simply a matter of going to the phone book, looking up the number under 'Clinton W.J and H' and giving him a call. It's a long process of finding someone who knows someone who knows someone and getting the ball rolling. As it turned out, someone else got to him first. An Australian Jewish organisation had arranged to bring him Down Under in May 2001 and approached me to organise one of the functions. I was disappointed not to be handling the entire tour, but I still jumped at the chance to be involved on even a minor level. Then, fate took a hand. Due to another commitment, President Clinton couldn't come in May, but he could in September. This didn't suit the Jewish organisation, but it suited me. In arranging my part of the original tour, I had begun building a relationship with President Clinton's agents in the US. With that tour now off and a window of opportunity presenting itself in September I made them an offer of three functions at US$150,000 each, a total of US$450,000 which, given the exchange rate at the time was close to AUD$900,000. Just like a year earlier when I had offered Nelson Mandela $1 million I didn't have, I didn't have the $900,000 for Bill Clinton lying around either but I was confident I could come up with it once we started selling tickets. All I needed was some 'seed money' to keep the ship afloat until the cash came rolling in.

You know that song, 'I get by with a little help from my friends'? I didn't write it, unfortunately, but I sing it a lot. The friend I went to on this occasion was a long-time supporter of mine named Grahame Mapp. As a matter of fact, when I started out in business on my own, Grahame let me use his boardroom as an office. Early every morning I would unpack my cardboard box full of pens, pencils, coffee cup and lists of possible leads to follow up, and sit at his boardroom table making calls until night-time when I would pack up my cardboard box and go home. (Unless of course Grahame wanted to hold a board meeting during the day, in which case I would pack up my cardboard box a lot earlier and make myself scarce for a few hours.) In the 20 or so years since then both our businesses had grown. Grahame started as an accountant but has since had enormous success as an investment banker, coal exporter, racehorse owner-breeder (he owns Hobartville Stud) and media owner. His company Omnilab has produced a number of successful movies and operates several Pay TV channels.

I got to know Grahame through the charitable organisation Variety Club and we'd see each other regularly at club functions and committee meetings. A special interest of Grahame's is the Children's Hospital at Westmead, so when I decided that the hospital would be the charity to benefit from President Clinton's opening function in Australia, he was the first person I contacted.

I asked Grahame if he would put up the money for the function. In return he would get a table of ten and I would pay him back as soon as the ticket money came in. He immediately agreed, but that wasn't the full extent of his generosity. At the auction on the night he paid $55,000 for a pristine 1948 Bradman's 'Invincibles' signed cricket bat and for good measure bought a teddy bear signed by President Clinton for another $25,000. Grahame, and hundreds of big-hearted guests like him, helped us raise over $1.2 million for the Children's Hospital at Westmead that night, but there was an awful lot of work that had to be done before we got to that point.

Organising a tour for an ex-US president is not all that different from organising a tour for a current US president. There are various protocols that have to be followed, plus strict arrangements have to be put in place to maintain security and ensure that the president doesn't in any way find himself in a place or a position that might not reflect well on the White House.

I'm an old hand at it now, but back then it was all very much a learning experience, and a fascinating one.

I contracted President Clinton for three functions to be held on 8, 9 and 10 September 2001. Factoring in the long flights from and to the US it was a gruelling three-day schedule, so it was arranged for him to unwind on the Great Barrier Reef on the fourth day. That's right, I was hosting Bill Clinton on 9/11, but we'll get to that later. First, I had to jump through some hoops in order to be authorised to arrange the tour at all.

In June, three months before Mr Clinton was due to arrive, a member of his staff flew into Sydney from the US to vet me and make sure I was who I said I was and not some nut-job trying an elaborate scam. I hosted him for a couple of days; showed him the sights, took him for a walk across the Sydney Harbour Bridge and to a flash seafood restaurant and I must have passed the test because he reported back to Washington that I seemed reasonably sane.

With the go ahead from the US, I ramped up the

planning. The first event was an enormous function at Randwick Racecourse to benefit the Children's Hospital at Westmead. The next day was a dinner, also in Sydney, for 40 people at $50,000 per head organised through John Robertson from the NSW Labour Council, and then we had a private function in Melbourne for 30 people at $20,000 each arranged by merchant banker and Liberal Party powerbroker Michael Kroger and his-then father-in-law Andrew Peacock.

Two weeks before Mr Clinton was due to arrive I received a call from the Attorney General's office in Canberra asking to have a meeting with me.

'Sure,' I said. 'Why?'

'Because you are bringing President Clinton to Australia,' they said as if I was an idiot.

We arranged to meet at the Stamford Plaza Hotel (now the Intercontinental) at Double Bay. Graeme Goldberg, the hotel manager, had rung me a month or two earlier and offered to provide complimentary accommodation for President Clinton. I said yes and he gave me the hotel's public relations business as well.

I arrived at the meeting 10 minutes late because… well, because I'm always 10 minutes late. I was expecting to meet one person but when I walked in there were 17 people waiting.

There were a couple from the Attorney General's office, some from the Federal police, the NSW police and the local police. There were people for risk assessment and people for security. I asked someone what they did and they said they were in charge of the motorcade.

'Motorcade?' I asked.

'Of course,' they said. 'Wherever President Clinton goes he has to have a motorcade.'

Then there were five big guys in blue suits wearing sunglasses and clear plastic earphones.

'Don't tell me,' I joked. 'You're the Secret Service.'

'Yes,' said one without smiling. 'The rest of us will get here later.'

It's amazing to watch the Secret Service in action. They do everything so well. Nothing, and I mean nothing, is left to chance. Someone is in charge of every venue. There is a person where the event is, and a person at the nearest hospital. They know how long it takes to get from every place the president will be, to every place he has to go. They know the best route — and the alternative route in case that one is blocked. By the time President Clinton arrived — with another 10 Secret Service men — they knew more about the roads of Sydney and Melbourne than I will ever know.

And how much did this all cost me? Not a cent. The US government paid for everything. They even flew their Pacific area chief John Johnson in from Hawaii to oversee the operation.

And that's all before the Advance Man hits town. The Advance Man is worth a chapter on his own. His name is Mort Engelberg and he has been with Bill Clinton since he was Governor of Arkansas. It is a labour of love for Mort, he doesn't get paid for being the President's Advance Man. Not that he needs the money. He is very successful in his own right as a film producer. He produced *The Big Easy* with Dennis Quaid and the *Smokey and the Bandit* movies, amongst others.

Mort's brother was doing some work for Bill Clinton in the late 1980s, and when then-Governor Clinton decided to run for the presidency Mort offered to provide his show business expertise for the campaign. Mort is a lovely guy and a great storyteller. He has some amazing memories of life on the campaign trail with Bill and Hillary. When Bill announced he was seeking the Democratic nomination, it didn't exactly set the world on fire. The campaign team consisted of Bill, Mort and another guy. They would walk through airports on their way to out of town speaking engagements and no one would raise an eyebrow. Nothing much was happening for them, but the momentum built slowly and gained speed until Bill and his running mate Al Gore won the nomination and set their sights on the White House. Mort tells a beautiful story about how he had this great idea to hire a bus, put Bill and Hillary Clinton and Al and Tipper Gore in it and just start driving, stopping to speak to whoever was interested. Mort's plan was to hire the bus for three days, but it was so successful that they just kept going for three weeks. They were stopping 12 times a day, attracting crowds of up to 10,000 people. If they were running late, the people would just wait. Mort tells of the bus driving into some little town at midnight and the headlights illuminating a giant crowd of thousands of people waiting in the dark to hear what Bill had to say. The way Mort tells it, you can just see it, like a scene out of one of his movies.

Mort always arrives a week before President Clinton, and he then walks every step that the president is going to take when he is in town. That's not a figure of speech by the way. When I say Mort walks every step, I mean he walks every step — and I walk it with him. Bill Clinton likes to shop, so if there is a shop I think he might be interested in, Mort and I will walk in so he can have a look around. The same with any restaurant that he might dine in. Mort and I will go and have a meal so he can see if it is up to the required standard (I must say that's probably my favourite part of the process) and we will drive the routes that the motorcade will take. Before that first tour, Mort and I also took a ride on a Rivercat so he could check out the waterways between Sydney Harbour and the Parramatta River.

My role at this point is to teach Mort about the cities that President Clinton will be visiting, but in the 16 years that I have known him I've also learnt an awful lot from Mort. Because of his movie background, Mort has great insight into what will make the best angle for the TV cameras, or where we should set up a photo for the press. More importantly, he also knows better than most where a photo should *not* be taken. Press photographers are great. I love them. I wouldn't be a success in the publicity business if it wasn't for them, but that doesn't mean I ever relax when I am around them. If they see an opportunity for a quirky shot that their picture editor will plaster all over page one, they'll take it — no matter if it puts my client in a less than favourable light. Often, it's not what is going on in the foreground of the shot that grabs their attention, it's what they see — and everyone else misses — that is in the background. How often have you seen a picture of a campaigning politician smiling innocently in front of a sign that says 'Exit' or 'This Way Out'? One of the most famous political photos of all time was the one taken of 1952 US presidential candidate Adlai Stevenson during his campaign against Dwight D. 'Ike' Eisenhower. Stevenson was sitting in a chair reading, with one leg crossed over the other when an eagle-eyed photographer noticed he had a big hole in the sole of his shoe. He got down low, snapped the shot and the picture went around the world. The Eisenhower camp even had campaign buttons made up with an image of the hole in the shoe and the words, 'Don't Let This Happen To You — Vote for Ike'.

Needless to say, I never want to see something like that happen to someone I am representing, and having a pro like Mort around to provide a very astute second pair of eyes is priceless. I even ring him from time to time for advice on good photo opportunities, such as when I was doing some work with Prime Minister Tony Abbott.

With all the advance work done, the security in place, the routes for the motorcade okay-ed and a very nice lunch at the Sydney Fish Markets enjoyed, it was finally time for President Clinton's arrival. It was the first time I got to meet him, but we had already had contact. I had been in an Indigenous arts and crafts shop in North Queensland a few weeks earlier and spotted an Aboriginal saxophone. Now I know what you're thinking 'isn't the right term for an Aboriginal saxophone a didgeridoo?' Not this time. It was a carved wooden saxophone painted with traditional Indigenous dots and patterns. It was pretty spectacular and the first three words that came to my mind when I saw it were, 'Saxophone. Bill. Clinton'. I bought it and sent it to him express post in time for his birthday on 19 August. He wrote a nice note thanking me and saying how he was looking forward to meeting me. The letter arrived at my office before I was back from my trip and my staff had it framed, along with a picture of Mr Clinton playing a real saxophone (I don't think he'd get much sound out of the wooden one) waiting for me when I returned. It was the first of dozens of letters that have passed between the two of us since that day. I often send him a card and present — usually a tie — on his birthday, and he always replies. He even wears the ties.

You know the closing line of the movie *Casablanca* when Humphrey Bogart's character Rick stands at the airport and says, 'I think this is the beginning of a beautiful friendship'? Well, that's how it was for me, waiting with Mort in the VIP room at Sydney Airport on 8 September, when President Clinton's flight touched down. Back then, when he was just starting to make his first foray into the corporate world, he flew commercial. Before long, it was private jets all the way. He travels pretty light. Just him, a friend or two and about a dozen Secret Service men. Over the years President Clinton would bring numerous people as guests on his trips Down Under. One time it was Mike Penn, the former Microsoft executive who worked for six years as pollster to President Clinton and was Hillary Clinton's chief strategist when she ran for the Democratic nomination in 2008. Others times he brought Phillip Levine who is now the Mayor of Miami; Vinod Gupta, the Indian born American businessman and philanthropist, Frank Giustra, the merchant banker who founded Lionsgate movie studio, and Aram Glazer, whose family owns Manchester United football club. On that first tour it was Joe Lockhart, his former press secretary.

When President Clinton and his party arrived, they came straight into the VIP area where Mort introduced me to him. He gave me a warm handshake. We made some small talk and then he said, 'I'd like to go for a walk'.

We walked back into the baggage collection area, me on one side of him, Mort on the other, with two Secret Service people a couple of paces in front and all the others trailing behind. When we stopped, they stopped, when we started up again, they started up again. It must have been quite a sight. People waiting to collect their bags were standing around with their mouths open, not quite believing what they were seeing.

'Do you have a phone?' Bill asked me. 'I'd like to call Hillary and Chelsea to let them know I arrived ok.'

I pulled out my phone and the former President of the United States gave me his home telephone number so I could dial the former First Lady for him. I still have the number. I won't make that old joke about 'I could give it to you, but I'd have to kill you' because it's not true. That's what we have Secret Service people for.

After Bill had spoken to Hillary he handed back my phone and said, 'I think we should turn back now.'

Sounds simple, but there is an art to this. When Bill Clinton turns around to walk in the opposite direction, it's not just a case of, well, turning around and walking in the opposite direction. The formation has to stay intact, so Bill, Mort and I slowed down and turned in a slow arc with all the others swinging around us, like a gate. It was like a chorus line number from a Busby Berkeley musical.

We motorcaded it back to the hotel and people were everywhere: TV crews, press, public... everyone wanted to get a picture or just a look at the former Most Powerful Man in The World. Unsurprisingly the hotel had given us the Presidential Suite, which included a room for Mr Clinton's right-hand man Doug Band.

Doug has been an advisor to President Clinton since the White House days. He is the one who set up the Clinton Global Initiative, a charitable organisation that employs 1,000 people and does amazing work around the world, including the fighting of AIDS in Africa and Asia.

I had a load of items I wanted signed by President Clinton, like posters of him to be auctioned, and a box of Cuban cigars I wanted to give to him, all set up in Doug's room.

When I'm going through it with Doug, Bill sticks his head in and says, 'do you want me to do that signing now?' so we take everything into the main suite and he's sitting there signing. He says, 'These are nice posters.' I tell him I got them from the US Embassy. I don't tell him they were going to throw them out because they'd just got the new batch with George W. Bush on them. When I give him the box of Cuban cigars Doug Band asks, 'Can you accept those Mr President?'

'I couldn't back in the States,' he says. 'But here it's fine.'

'In that case,' I say, pulling out another box, 'could you sign this one for me too?'

He does, and I still have it in my office.

Speaking of Cuba, one of the posters I ask Mr Clinton to sign is a JFK election poster from 1960 with the slogan 'Vote 1 Kennedy'. As he is signing it he says, 'You know, when I was still in office I was at the United Nations General Assembly and I was standing at the end of this long line shaking hands with everyone. There was a large Namibian official who I shook hands with and when he stepped aside I'm face to face with Fidel Castro. He puts his hand out and says' 'I hope this isn't going to embarrass you President Clinton, but I want to pay my respects to you before you leave office'. I said 'not at all' and shook hands with him, becoming the first President to do so in over forty years. I got on really well with Castro. I think I could have done a deal with him to fix things.'

Then he points to the Kennedy poster and says, 'He hated Kennedy. After the Bay of Pigs, the Democrats only had 15 per cent of the vote in Florida. My last election I had 47 per cent.'

The signing all done, it was time to hit the road. Or more accurately, the water. A mobile phone-internet provider company had sponsored the first event for $143,000 and the owner had provided his luxury boat to transport the president and his entourage across the harbour and up Parramatta River to visit the Children's Hospital at Westmead. To get to the boat we went out the back door of the hotel, down a laneway and along the beach at Double Bay. It was a similar scene to the stroll at the airport: President Clinton at the front of an arrowhead formation with the Secret Service fanned out behind, and a phalanx of photographers walking backwards, snapping away, in front. As this strange procession of about 20 people made its way across Double Bay beach there was a lady sitting on a bench reading a book. She didn't even look up as the president passed her. One of the press photographers took a fantastic shot of the woman engrossed in her book unaware of who was walking by and it was published on the front page of the next morning's *Sun Herald*.

We didn't have a motorcade on the harbour. We had a boat-a-cade, with an escort of police boats all around us. On the way there I had the opportunity to have a good chat with Mr Clinton. I asked him what his plans were for the future. At that time, he had spent the previous 24 years in public service, first as Attorney General, and then Governor of Arkansas, earning around $30,000 a year, and two terms as President earning $250,000 a year. He had left office owing $8 million in legal bills. He told me his first priority was to provide for his family.

'I have to do events like this to make some money so, God forbid, if anything happens to me Hillary and Chelsea will be okay,' he said. 'The home will be paid off, we won't have any debt and then, I want to start giving back. I want to do some good.'

When you think about it, there aren't really many politicians in the world who can fix things. When someone is in office, like say Donald Trump, Scott Morrison or Theresa May, they spend as much time playing politics as they do running their country or looking at international issues. There is always public service — no one would put themselves and their families through what they are subjected to without a genuine belief that they can make a difference — but there is also the shadow of being toppled from power by the opposition, or their own party.

At the time that President Clinton left office, apart from Nelson Mandela, there was probably no one in the world who had the cache to do the good that he did, and that's how the Clinton Global Initiative and Clinton Foundation came about.

When we arrived at the Children's Hospital I had arranged for some celebrities and well-known athletes including dual Olympic Gold medallist Michael Diamond, marathon swimmer Susie Maroney and high-profile radio broadcaster Jackie O, to be there to provide photo opportunities before we went inside. As Bill went around the wards and met the children, parents and staff, we allowed access to one photographer, who then made their pictures available to everyone else. The country's biggest selling newspaper, *The Sunday Telegraph* had a shot of President Clinton with one of the patients on their front page.

The boat trip on the way back to Double Bay was one of the great memories of my life. As we sat there, eating lollies and shooting the breeze, I asked him if he had a dream of what he'd like to do some time in the future.

'Max,' he said. 'I'm just looking forward to the time

when I can sit on a park bench with Hillary and no one bothers us.'

I immediately started singing, 'When I get older, losing my hair, many years from now...' and he sang along. There we were: the showman's son from Bournemouth and the ex-leader of the free world, sitting on a boat singing a Beatles' song. Who'd have thought?

Back at the hotel we caught the motorcade to Randwick Racecourse for the biggest event of the trip, a 1,000-guest dinner, at $10,000 a table of ten, or $25,000 a VIP table of ten that included a handshake and photo with the president. It all went very well — except for a minor glitch.

One of the big moments of the function was when the great Australian soprano Marina Prior, star of *Phantom of the Opera*, sang the National Anthem. Or it would have been, if the PA system didn't go on the blink from, 'let us rejoice...' and keep going in and out all the way to 'advance Australia fair...' Marina hung in there like a trouper, but what should have been a stirring rendition of our national song sounded like a dodgy transistor radio on a building site. I haven't seen Marina since.

National Anthem aside, the function was a roaring success. I had rung John Symond from Aussie Home Loans and asked if he wanted to introduce President Clinton on the night. He said sure. I said, 'thanks. Oh, by the way, it'll cost you a $25,000 table and a $50,000 donation'. Julia Ross, the human resources magnate, paid the same amount to offer the thanks at the end of the night. Entrepreneur Jim Byrnes rang and asked if I wanted a three-bedroom apartment to auction. It wasn't built yet, but if we paid him his costs of $190,000, anything over that was ours. I said ok, hoping we could get $191,000 for it. As an aside, Jim had bought an antique bible to give to President Clinton and was getting all Australia's living prime ministers to sign it. Everything went well until he got to Paul Keating, who flatly refused. Apparently, they had a ding-dong argument over the phone before Mr Keating finally came around.

With Ray Hadley as auctioneer the apartment sold for $370,000. In keeping with the Children's Hospital theme, we had a giant teddy bear sitting on stage. Hadley asked President Clinton if he'd come up and sign it, which he did, and Grahame Mapp snapped it up for $25,000. Grahame also paid $55,000 for a cricket bat I'd bought from Christies for $7,000. The money just kept rolling in, which brings us to another little glitch.

Remember the mobile phone-internet guy who sponsored the event and lent us his boat? Well, turns out he wasn't all he made out to be. As sponsor of the function he got to sit next to the guest of honour, and when a beautiful framed photo and autograph of Mahatma Gandhi came up for auction, he promptly bought it for $55,000 and presented it to President Clinton, who took it back to the US with him. Six months later, when the phone guy's house of cards collapsed and the authorities started seizing his assets, they somehow found reference to the $55,000 picture of Mahatma Gandhi and started proceedings to get it back. I'm not sure how it ended up. I didn't like to ask.

It was an amazing night. Laurence Fishburne and Carrie-

Anne Moss were in town filming *The Matrix*, so they were there, along with heaps of local celebrities. The mood in the room was amazing and we raised $1.2 million for the Children's Hospital, but I remember when we got back to the hotel that night feeling a little down. Maybe it was just because I'd been on such a high, but at the time I thought we might have raised more. It's only now when I think back on it that I realise what an incredible achievement it had been, not just to raise that much money in one night, but to pull the whole thing together at all.

The next day we went and played golf. President Clinton had played at the New South Wales Golf Club with Greg Norman when he was still in office and liked it so much that he wanted to go back, so I organised it. I'm no golfer, so for me it was a nice stroll, but President Clinton must have enjoyed it, because when I visited him in his New York office about six months later, there on a shelf was a framed photo of us all leaning on our golf clubs taken on the day.

That night we had the private function for 40 people at $50,000 a head. I think the most excited man in the room that night was NSW Labor premier Bob Carr. When President Clinton walked in, Carr said to me, 'Max, you're a genius!' Bob is a noted student of US political history. The chance to shoot the breeze with a former president was his idea of heaven.

The next day we flew to Melbourne in a couple of private planes arranged by the mobile phone guy. Incidentally, that guy was so pumped by spending time with President Clinton for a few days that he approached Mort with a brilliant idea.

He wanted to make a movie. He'd pay President Clinton $5 million to star in it, and give Mort $250,000 just to get him to agree. Mort, ever the gentleman, asked the phone guy what the movie would be about.

'It'll be *The Godfather IV*,' he said. Needless to say, it never got the green light.

The Melbourne function, in a beautiful villa at the top of Crown Casino, was another great success, and that was the end of the formal part of President Clinton's trip. To help him wind down after the three frantic days, he was booked into a resort at Port Douglas for a few days lying around the pool before the long flight back to the States. Solomon Lew had given us his plane for the trip to Queensland and I said my goodbyes to President Clinton in Melbourne. It had been an incredible experience that we had both enjoyed and we said we should do it again some time. I waved him off and that, I thought, was that. I got home to Sydney, had a nice meal and went to bed looking forward to my first sleep-in for months.

I was awoken by the sound of my two mobile phones ringing and beeping at the same time. Text messages were coming in by the second. My landline was buzzing and there was a banging on the door. It was 11 September 2001. America was under attack and every reporter in the country wanted to know where Bill Clinton was.

Any thoughts of a leisurely time in the sun went straight out of the window. The Secret Service closed in around President Clinton, while at the same time President George W. Bush signed a special order to dispatch a military aircraft from Guam to Cairns to pick up his predecessor and then, with all US airspace closed down, allow it to land at La Guardia Airport in New York.

My three days with the president had ended in the most dramatic of circumstances, but there was a postscript.

In 2006 I was at the World Business Forum at Radio City Music Hall in New York. It is a very big annual event, and I had taken a group of 25 Australian business people. The guest speaker was President Clinton. I was sitting in the front row with my people, and he was standing on stage giving his address. At the end there was a question and answer. Someone asked if the president remembered where he was when he heard about 9/11.

'I sure do,' he said pointing down at me. 'I was in Australia with this guy... Max Markson!'

And that's what I call a name-check.

CHAPTER 3
ON THE ROAD WITH BILL CLINTON

When President Clinton and his entourage flew back to the US I sat down, took a deep breath and thought, 'what am I going to do with my life now?' And then it dawned on me. Bring him back again.

That first tour had gone so well, and I had enjoyed Mr Clinton's company so much, that I couldn't imagine anything else topping that experience. It was also true that I had taken him only to Sydney and Melbourne. There were a lot of people throughout the country (and, as it turned out, New Zealand) who hadn't had the opportunity to get close to him, and a lot more money to be raised for charity. I got straight back onto his people and said, 'why don't we do it all again' and they said sure.

Within five months Mort is back at Sydney Airport waiting for the president to walk through the doors of customs.

I would have been there with him, but I was already in Perth getting ready for the first of what would be five gigs in eight days. The first trip it had taken me a few days to break the ice and get to know President Clinton and for him to get to know me and my, sometimes, unusual ways. This time there was none of that. We picked up where we had left off, and on this trip and the tours that followed, we had some unforgettable experiences and memories that I will take with me forever.

It all started on the first leg of the tour in Perth. There we were at Coco's, a fabulous restaurant overlooking the river. Just an intimate little group: me, the 42nd President of the United States, Mr Clinton's right-hand man Doug Band, Alan Jones, Brian Doyle and a couple of people from the Princess Margaret Children's Hospital. Oh, and about 15 Secret Service men and a dozen West Australian and Australian Federal Police. The ones of us without guns are sitting at a table out on the patio, with the Secret Service and police fanned out around the building and on the roadway. Brian asks President Clinton how he copes with all the security around him all the time. He shrugs and says it's just a way of life for him. Just months after 9/11, the Americans were hunting Osama Bin Laden and Bill knew only too well that he would have been on al-Qaeda's hit list as well. I don't know about Brian, but I was very happy to have the Secret Service keeping an eye on us.

We had a wonderful meal, the food was excellent, the wine was flowing and we decided to have one more drink before heading back to the casino where we were staying. Brian excused himself to go to the men's room. Now when it comes to practical jokes, I have the mental age of an eight-year-old. 'Quick', I said, 'let's hide'. President Clinton says, 'you're on' and jumps up. We all run to the side of the terrace and crouch down behind some giant pot-plants, about 10 of us, and the Secret Service.

I'm not sure if President Clinton had played hide-and-seek for a while, but he seemed to enjoy it. Brian came back, saw the empty table, looked around, swore, and started walking out. We all jumped up laughing and yelling, 'we're here'. Brian was not impressed. That's the trouble with comedians. No sense of humour.

The next night we had a big charity fundraising function for the Women's and Children's Hospital in Adelaide. We flew straight there from Perth but President Clinton wanted to see Uluru, so he took a detour in a private plane and met up with us for the gig. As always Brian is in good form up on stage and finishes his act by saying, 'It's come to this. I'm now the warm-up guy for an amateur saxophone player. Last night in Perth President Clinton cost me a beer'. He then looks down at the president and says, 'You owe me a beer you know'.

The following day there was a day off in Adelaide. I'd organised for President Clinton to meet Russell Crowe later in the week. Russell's movie *A Beautiful Mind* had just come out and I thought I'd better organise a screening of it. In the end the meeting with Russell Crowe didn't happen but we did get to see the movie. When it was over President Clinton said, 'Brian, I owe you that beer. Let's go back to the hotel and I'll buy you one'. We go back to the hotel in the motorcade — as you do — and have a beer in the bar.

Next stop is Melbourne and Brian gets up on stage doing his act. President Clinton thinks Brian is hilarious by the way. By now he's writing down Brian's jokes to tell to his staff when he gets back to the States. So, Brian gets to the 'warm-up guy for an amateur saxophone player' bit and this time he says, 'President Clinton, you cost me a beer in Perth, you bought me a beer in Adelaide. But the beer I missed out on in Perth was a Crown Lager and the one you bought me in Adelaide was a VB. A Crown Lager costs eight dollars and the VB was four dollars and so, Mr President, you owe me four bucks.'

That night we were staying at the Crown Casino. They have a cigar bar there called Fidel's, where they have karaoke. Needless to say, I love karaoke. Apart from hiding from my friends behind pot plants it's one of my favourite things to do. I've arranged for us all to go there after the function and invite President Clinton along. He says he'll be there. When we arrive at the hotel a few of us, including Brian and some off duty Secret Service men, head straight to the bar. At about midnight I ring President Clinton's room and tell Doug Band we're just about to start singing and do they want to join us? Doug says, 'Oh, we're in for the night now, thanks anyway, but have a good time.' We push on regardless. We're right into it, singing away, having a great time and somehow I hear my phone ringing. It's the president and he says, 'we're coming down'. I tell the others and the off-duty Secret Service guys jump up and say, 'we've got to go right now. We can't be here socialising when the president is here'. They hot-foot it out of there and next thing, Mr Clinton walks in with his 12-man on-duty Secret Service detail. Without missing a beat, he goes straight over to Brian Doyle and hands him one, two, three, four US dollar bills. He signs one of them and says, 'I bet Max will want to auction this.' Brian replied 'Well he's not getting it!'

After that President Clinton stayed with us and we did

karaoke till the wee hours. He wanted to sing The Beatles, Joe Cocker and Elton John songs. We sung heaps of Beatles songs including All You Need Is Love, Hey Jude, Joe Cocker's Up Where We Belong and Elton John's Candle in the Wind. It must have been three in the morning when we finally left. One of my fondest memories is standing on the little stage with President Clinton singing *New York, New York*. I also remember the two of us singing The Beatles' *In My Life*. He told me it had just been voted one of the five best written songs of all time.

He might be an amateur saxophone player, but he knows his music.

Our next stop was Brisbane. It was a big function at the Sheraton Hotel (now the Sofitel) for the Royal Children's Hospital. On the morning Doug asked me, 'Do you mind if we are late tonight?' I asked 'what's happening?' and he said, 'Oh, the president just has to meet the Queen'. Turned out Her Majesty was in town for the CHOGM meeting. As a good British lad, I gave my permission. I guess my knighthood is still in the mail.

There were a couple of memorable moments that night. The first was when Sarina Russo, one of Queensland's most successful businesswomen, was accompanying President Clinton to his table. Sarina had paid a small fortune to be major sponsor of the event and she and I were walking him past the silent auction items on our way to the main function room when he noticed a framed *Casablanca* movie poster with signatures of Humphrey Bogart and Ingrid Bergman.

'That's nice,' he said.

'Oh Mr President,' Sarina said, 'I'll buy it for you.'

She turned to me. 'How much Max?'

'$5,000,' I said and took it out of the sale.

That must have been the most expensive 50 metre walk of Sarina's life.

The other thing I remember wasn't as nice. For the first and only time on our tours together, President Clinton was heckled. It was when he had just got up to give his speech and a rather red-faced gentleman who had obviously been enjoying the hospitality a little too much started shouting out disparaging comments about America's involvement in the Vietnam War. Mr Clinton allowed him to have his say and then replied calmly and politely.

The man wouldn't give up, continuing to shout over the top of President Clinton and becoming increasing belligerent. It was then that the Secret Service men rolled into action.

Have you ever wondered how the Secret Service deals with someone who is shouting abuse at a former US president? No, they don't shoot him, much as they'd probably like to. In fact, it was handled so quickly and efficiently that I felt like applauding. Everyone else did.

Four of them simply walked up behind him and two tipped his chair backwards so he couldn't stand up. The other two then lifted the front legs of the chair and the four of them carried him out of the room. He was last seen being escorted down the escalators and deposited gently, still in his chair, at the cab rank outside. It was one of the best performances of the night.

After Brisbane, we went back to Sydney. When we got there Doug Band said to me, 'We've had a great week. We'd like to throw you a party to say thanks. Do think you could organise it?' I said sure, we can do it at the hotel after the show.

That night we had 2,500 people for dinner at the Convention and Exhibition Hall at Darling Harbour. Afterwards we went back to the hotel and President Clinton was having a long chat to Brian, who he really likes. Brian is telling him his life story and how he grew up in Dublin. President Clinton asks if he has any family still there. Brian says he has a brother.

'Give me his details,' he says. 'I'm going to Dublin soon. I'll look him up and say hello.'

That night we have a nice party at the hotel. I pay for it all, but the next day Doug comes up and says to me, 'Who paid for the party last night?' I tell him that I did, but not to worry about it. He wouldn't hear of it. He told me that President Clinton insisted that he would pay, and he handed me a credit card and told me to charge the party to it, which I thought was pretty impressive.

That same day we had arranged to play golf, and a guy called Steven from Darwin had paid $20,000 for charity the night before to play a round with President Clinton. Now I'm no golfer, but this guy was even worse than me. He hacked his way around the course, with the former President of the United States giving him lessons all the way. President Clinton is no pro, but he loves his golf and

I'm not sure if he thought he could help this guy or whether he just felt he should get his $20,000 worth. Either way he now has a story to tell for the rest of his life.

We rushed straight from the golf course to the airport and I waved them off back to the States.

Three months later I get a phone call at 4 o'clock in the afternoon from Doug Band.

'Max,' he says. 'Remember President Clinton said he'd look up Brian Doyle's brother? Well, we're in Dublin. The boss wonders if you'd be good enough to track him down for us and invite him and his family to the Four Seasons Hotel at lunchtime.'

Well, I found Brian's brother's number and gave him a call. After finally convincing him I wasn't some madman trying to sell him some aluminium siding, or whatever the equivalent is in Ireland, he told me he'd love to meet President Clinton, and so would all his other relatives. I told him to make sure to take a camera. I believe they had a wonderful time. Unfortunately, the camera didn't work. No problem. President Clinton arranged for some photos to be taken and he had them sent to Brian's family when he got back to the US.

If you ever want to know what sort of person Bill Clinton is, I think that story says it all. I couldn't wait to work with him again and, happily, it didn't take long. I got a call from BMW New Zealand asking if I could arrange a function over there with President Clinton for the end of May 2002. Sticking to my policy of never saying no to anything, I agreed. Luckily Mr Clinton was heading back into the general vicinity anyway as part of the rescheduling of his engagements in Asia following 9/11 and we could arrange a trip to fit in with his plans. His people also asked if I could arrange a private function while he was there to help raise funds for his library. All presidents open a library after they have been in office, but they have to pay for it themselves. Barack Obama's library will cost the best part of a billion dollars and I would guess Bill Clinton's would have been around half of that, so it was no mean feat to come up with the money.

Just like I had with Nelson Mandela, I decided to organise a reception for 20 wealthy New Zealanders at $25,000 a head. Only problem is, I didn't know 20 wealthy New Zealanders. I didn't even know 20 poor New Zealanders. I'd never set foot in the country in my life. Even so, I flew over to Auckland, booked into the Hilton Hotel in Auckland and asked the concierge to find me a copy of the New Zealand version of the BRW Rich List. When he did I gave him fifty bucks and said, 'Do me a favour. Get me as many phone numbers for these people as you can'. The next morning he gave me the list and I started cold calling. Within a few days I'd sold the 20 tickets and the best part of $500,000 was headed to the Clinton Foundation to help with the cost of the library.

Peter O'Keefe from the Clinton Foundation came over for the function and told me about a guy called Terry McAuliffe. He would go on to become Governor of Virginia, but at the time he was the chief fundraiser for President Clinton and had raised hundreds of millions of dollars for both his election campaigns and the Foundation.

'Wow,' I thought. 'Imagine how much I could learn from this guy.' I asked Peter if there was any way I could meet with Terry McAuliffe the next time I was in the States. He said he'd organise it.

The big moment came a few months later in July when I was in New York and I met Terry at the New York Hilton when he was attending a National Democratic Committee conference. This was my big chance. Here I was, with one of the biggest fundraisers in the world. I took a deep breath and asked him to impart the wisdom that had taken him to the top of mountain.

'How do you do it?' I said. 'What is your secret?'

'I just ask,' he said. 'The worst they can do is say no.'

That same trip to New York I spent some time with President Clinton and got an insight into just what a great support he is to Hillary in her political career. President Clinton and Doug invited me along to a party they were going to. The party was for Hillary Clinton's personal adviser Huma Abedin's birthday. Before we left Doug and I were sitting in the rear of the car waiting while President Clinton was talking with Hillary's speech writer who was showing him a speech he had written for Hillary to give the next day. President Clinton was going through it, line by line, making suggestions, deleting and inserting sections and generally giving it the full benefit of his experience. When the speech writer left the car, Bill immediately rang Hillary and told her the changes he had made and the suggestions he thought would make it better. He was like, 'I've done this and that and I think you'll get a lot of oxygen from this...' Here he was, a former president, but more importantly, a husband, giving serious time to his wife's work and caring very deeply about how she went. It was a very interesting behind-the-scenes view of one of the world's biggest power couples in action.

That was my first experience of being with President Clinton in the US. Over the years I have been able to host him in Australia, and I have always given my absolute all to ensure that his trips have not only been successful financially for local charities and his foundation, but also enjoyable and something he will always remember fondly. In return he has always been incredibly hospitable to me and given me some amazing memories on my visits to America.

Often when I go to New York I go up to his office and meet him or his staff — I even took my mother up there once — and whenever he invites me to one of his major events I hop straight on a plane and get over there.

In February 2004 I was invited to the opening of the Clinton Library in his home town of Little Rock. Just me and about 30,000 other people. I flew in and checked into the Peabody Hotel, where he was staying. When I told Doug Band that I was there he said, 'the President says you must come and have dinner with us tonight'. So there we were, about eight of us having dinner in President Clinton's suite. What did we eat? Take-away.

That night President Clinton was asking me about my plans for the week. I told him I'd like to go to Hope, where he was born and grew up, so he arranged for one of his people to take me for a drive out there. If ever you want to know how far this man has come in his life, you have to go to Hope. I don't know how to describe it, other than to say think of the lowest socio-economic area you've ever seen and then drop it down a few notches. You drive through slums to get there, and it doesn't improve when you arrive. It is just incredible that he could go from there to the White House.

After the official opening of the library, which included Presidents Carter, Bush Snr, the current President George W. Bush, Hillary Clinton and Bono and The Edge from U2 performing, I was invited to the luncheon. This was a far more intimate affair. Probably only 1,500 people. I was sitting next to some congressman but all around me it was a who's who. Morgan Freeman was there, Barbra Streisand, Kevin Spacey and Robin Williams. I shook hands with Eunice Kennedy and Teddy Kennedy. At the end of the day I walked back into town and found myself falling into step with a nice friendly couple by the name of Ted Danson and Mary Steenburgen.

The next year he launched his Clinton Global Initiative and every year since he has held a three-day event which is one of the biggest meetings of political, financial and philanthropic movers and shakers in the world. It is a way for some of the wealthiest and most important people to get together with the heads of the charities that the Clintons support. It is also a celebrity-spotter's dream.

That first year I bumped into Mick Jagger, another time I was walking along and Brad Pitt passed me going in the opposite direction. I told him, 'Love your work'. He turned back and said, 'I only like about half of it'. One time I was having a sing-along with Ted Turner, another I was sitting next to the former IRA boss Gerry Adams who showed me photos of his grandchildren.

The most unreal memory I have of a Clinton Global Initiative function was at a dinner at The Sheraton Hotel in New York. I am sitting at my table, with my back to the stage and look around. Behind me, in the front row is President Clinton and Hillary with King Abdullah and Queen Rania of Jordan. I look to the right and at another table there is Colin Powell deep in conversation with Barbra Streisand. At another table is Madeleine Albright and Daryl Hannah. I look to the left and Richard Branson is sitting with John Glenn. At the same table is Elvis Costello who is looking up at his wife Diana Krall performing on stage. It is the same everywhere I look.

I was the only person in the room I didn't know.

It is an amazing world that Bill Clinton inhabits. I'm just so grateful that he has let me in.

CHAPTER 4
THE PRESIDENT, THE VICE PRESIDENT AND FAT TONY
GEORGE BUSH SNR AND AL GORE (2001, 2007)

Bill Clinton wasn't the only ex-president that I hosted. Soon after I had waved President Clinton goodbye after his first visit in September 2001 I was contacted by his agents.

'You did such a good job with President Clinton,' they said. 'How would you like to put some speaking engagements together for President Bush?'

Given that President Bush had a bit on his plate at that time following 9/11 I thought that would be a bit difficult but then it turned out they were talking about the other President Bush, George Senior. Apparently that President Bush was going to be in Australia in November as part of a global corporate initiative put together by the Carlyle Group, one of the world's largest private equity and investment firms. Given that as he was going to be here anyway, I wouldn't have to arrange his transport or security — and the fact that I had got used to travelling in motorcades, I thought, 'why not?'

We arranged a function to benefit The Children's Hospital at Westmead and Sudden Infant Death Syndrome (SIDS) in the ballroom of Sydney's Wentworth hotel, where Princess Diana had danced with New South Wales Premier

Neville Wran in 1996. President Bush's office asked me to put together a list of topics that he should speak about. I felt he should talk about the effects of 9/11 and what advice he had given to his son George W. Bush on how to handle the crisis. I also suggested he answer criticism that he should have gone all the way to Baghdad and taken Saddam out during the first Gulf War.

I have to say I found him very easy to deal with and very open in the way he spoke both privately and at the function. The first time we actually met was when I arrived during the photo line. I had intended to be there a lot earlier but as usual I was late and President Bush was halfway through the photo line when I rushed into the room. He wasn't fazed at all and had handled it without missing a beat. Still, I suppose when you've been head of the CIA and President of the United States, having to get started on a photo line without your host there to hold your hand isn't going to put you off your game too much.

He told some nice little stories about his life in and out of the White House. He often mentioned his wife Barbara and you could see what a good team they were. One of the stories he told was how on the day that George W. had become governor of Texas and another son Jeb had become governor of Florida, he and Barbara had chartered a plane so they could congratulate them both on the same night, stopping first in Tallahassee and then Austin. At one of the stops there was a big media gathering and a journalist asked him how it felt to have two sons become governor on the same day. He said he answered, 'This is the happiest day of my life', and Barbara dug him in the ribs and said 'What about the day we got married?'

The consummate politician, he immediately answered, 'Wait on I haven't finished. I was about to say, apart from the day Barbara and I were married.'

My favourite story was how one morning earlier in the year he and Barbara had been at the family compound at Walker's Point in the state of Maine.

'George comes into our bedroom puts his feet up on the table and starts reading the morning paper,' he said. 'Barbara said "take your feet off the table". I said to her, "Barbara, he is the President of the United States" and she said, "I don't care who he is. George W. take your feet off the table".'

Off course I had to ask.

'What did he do?'

He answered, 'Took his feet off the table of course. Wouldn't you if your mother told you to?'

As for those issues I had asked him to talk about at the function, he did a great job. When it came to the question about why he hadn't sent the troops into Baghdad, he used an expression that is fairly common now but I was hearing for the first time.

'It is true,' he said. 'People ask me all the time why I didn't do that and I always give them the same answer — it's easy to be a Monday morning quarterback.'

The function was a huge success. We raised about $250,000 for the Children's Hospital at Westmead and SIDS. We had some nice photos taken and I sent some copies to him in the States. He sent back a beautiful thank you letter. It always amazes me when such busy and important people still find time for the little courtesies of life. It's just so... what's the right word? Presidential.

Bill Clinton and George Bush Snr remain the only two US presidents that I have hosted in Australia thus far but I can boast a vice president, an Oscar winner, a Grammy winner, an Emmy winner and a Nobel Prize winner. In fact, they are all the same person: Al Gore.

Mr Gore had close links to both President Clinton and President Bush Snr. He had been vice president to Bill Clinton, and narrowly lost to President Bush's son George W. Bush in the 2000 election. He had been out of politics for six years when I was contacted by his agent — the same one who represented President Clinton and President Bush Snr — but that didn't mean he was out of the news. In fact, in 2007, Al Gore was better known around the world than he had ever been before, all thanks to his film *An Inconvenient Truth*.

The documentary, about Vice President Gore's one-man campaign to educate Americans about global warming, won two Academy Awards in 2006, with his acceptance speech beamed live to millions. When I was asked to set up some functions I jumped at the chance. We reached an agreement on four gigs — two on Friday 14 September in Sydney, and two in Melbourne on Friday 21 September.

The idea was he would do a lunchtime event and then another private event in each city. Friday is the best day for a lunchtime function and the reaction was huge when we announced the dates.

In Sydney we had arranged for the private event to be held to launch the new Futures Exchange, and the big lunchtime function at the Convention and Exhibition Centre at Darling Harbour. They both sold out within hours. The reaction was similar in Melbourne and everything was going perfectly when, two weeks out, I received an email from the agent. Sorry, they said, but Vice President Gore can't do the two events in Sydney as he has another commitment. They said they would give my money back and that when he arrived in Australia on Wednesday 19 September, he'd do a reception for free to make up for the inconvenience. Well, I had some inconvenient truth for them.

To say I wasn't keen to tell all the people who had already booked and paid that the gig was off — and give back all the money — is something of an understatement. Setting up a tour like this is a very involved and very costly exercise. I have to put on extra staff, travel around the country looking at venues and accommodation, pay advance booking fees and spend countless hours on the phone that would otherwise be spent drumming up business.

I sent back a very long, firm — some might say desperate — reply, stating my dissatisfaction with the situation, and suggesting that if Vice President Gore was getting into Sydney early enough to do a reception on the Wednesday, why couldn't he just do the two functions as originally agreed to instead.

Overnight they sent a reply. Yes, that would be fine. Vice President Gore would be happy to do the two functions on the Wednesday as planned. He was happy? I was ecstatic. As was becoming something of a habit with me and members of the Clinton administration, I rushed out and bought him a beautiful tie as a thankyou gift.

It was only a few days later that I found out what the other engagement was that was so important that it meant he couldn't do my gig. He had to receive an Emmy. Okay, I could live with that.

I met Vice President Gore in the private lounge at Sydney airport. He shook my hand and said, 'Thank you so much for that tie, and thank you for being able to move the dates around. It was amazing.'

I said, 'Well Mr Vice President, if you had a date with Angelina Jolie on a Friday night and she said she could only come on Wednesday night, you'd change your arrangements, wouldn't you? Well it's the same with you. When I told people that you couldn't come on Friday but you could come on Wednesday, they changed their arrangements.'

Vice President Gore's visit had been sponsored by Lexus who were just launching the world's first luxury hybrid. They had given us one to use and we were sitting in it headed to the InterContinental hotel when I asked him about the Emmy he had just won. He told me it was to do with something called Current TV, a public access system that his company had pioneered. I said, 'That sounds interesting. What is it?' It was then I learned that if you ask Vice President Gore a question about one of his pet projects make sure you have some time on your hands. He told me the history of communications going back to the

15th century and the invention of the printing press. It was fascinating and a privilege and honour to be educated by one of the most respected people in the world, but I must admit I'm still not too sure how it all worked. When there was a lull in the conversation I managed to open my mouth just long enough to put my foot in it.

I said to him, 'It's a pity you didn't win the presidency.' I suddenly felt very stupid so I bumbled on and said, 'I mean you wouldn't have made the mistakes that President Bush has made.' He said, 'No, but I would have made different ones.'

We got to the hotel and went up to his suite. He picked up the newspaper on the table, and there was a story quoting me about how Prime Minister John Howard had snubbed Al Gore. What had happened was that I had tried to invite Malcolm Turnbull along to the luncheon and he had said no. The closest I could get was Pru Goward, the Liberal MP, who was John Howard's advisor on the status of women. Pru said she would love to come to the event, but when the press reported that noted environmentalist Malcolm Turnbull had knocked back the chance to meet with Al Gore, Prime Minister Howard told Pru Goward she couldn't go either. That's how the 'Howard Snubs Gore' headlines had come about. When Vice President Gore asked me about it, what could I say? I'm a PR man, I was trying to promote his tour and, of course, I managed to get the word Lexus in there as well.

The two events in Sydney went off perfectly. We did the private launch at the Futures Exchange and then Eddie

Maguire was MC for the big lunchtime function at Darling Harbour. Eddie's introduction went something like, 'Well Mr Gore, you might have an Oscar and an Emmy, but I bet you haven't got a Logie like me'. Since then Mr Gore has also picked up a Grammy and the Nobel Prize, so although Eddie had one up on him at the time, I wouldn't rule out anything when it comes to Al Gore.

I had invited a number of big names and celebrities to the function. Bob Hawke, who had met Al Gore on an earlier visit, was there and also Toni Collette, who I arranged to meet with him backstage and have a photo taken. A guest of special significance for me was Anthony Pratt who, as head of the giant recycling firm Visy, had a great interest in the Gore message. As well as attending the Sydney and Melbourne functions, Anthony was also hosting a private brunch on Sunday in Melbourne at the Pratt family mansion Raheen. I had just started doing some PR for Anthony and Al Gore's visit was a major stepping stone to us developing a very close professional and personal relationship to the stage where we now take annual holidays together with our families.

I had asked Anthony if he would provide his plane to take Vice President Gore down to Melbourne for the second leg of the trip. He said unfortunately both the Visy jets were unavailable, but he offered to hire one for us. Then James Packer offered the use of his plane so I turned Anthony down. I couldn't believe it. Here I was knocking back billionaires offering to give me corporate jets.

We flew down to Melbourne in James's jet, enjoying a

three-course lunch on the way. As is always the case on these tours, it is during the travel periods that I get the chance to get to have a chat and build a relationship with 'the talent'. Talent probably sounds like a disrespectful term with which to describe a former Vice President of the United States, but when it comes to Al Gore it is totally apt. The man is quite amazing in the breadth and depth of his accomplishments. He is a politician, environmentalist, writer, filmmaker, successful entrepreneur and businessman, as well as being a devoted husband and father. Personally, I found him a very nice guy; very amenable and agreeable. He was always happy to do the signings and photographs and is an absolutely brilliant speaker. I think it is a real shame that the two best chances he had to become President didn't work out. The first, in 1992, because he pulled out of the race to spend time with his family after his son was hit by a car, the second in 2000 when the US Supreme Court decided in favour of George W. Bush in a contentious case over balloting regulations.

It was very fortunate for me that the Vice President's visit went so smoothly because unbeknown to him, soon after he arrived I had another job land in my lap.

Many people around the world know the name Al Gore. Not so many remember Fat Tony, but in September 2007 they were both very much on my mind.

It all started with a phone call from the US when we landed in Melbourne on Thursday afternoon. Gloria Allred, the high-profile lawyer renowned for cases involving women's rights, was representing a gentleman by the name of Anthony Berretto, better known by his professional name: Fat Tony.

Fat Tony was Britney Spears' former bodyguard, and the key witness in the court battle between Britney and her ex-husband Kevin Federline over custody of their two young sons Sean and Jayden.

Fat Tony made some sensational claims in the courtroom over Britney's bizarre lifestyle and personal habits, but he had a lot more that he wanted to tell — and sell — and somehow Ms Allred had got hold of my name and number.

Would I like to broker some deals? Sure, I said. Good, she said, you've got 48 hours to make it all happen.

Even before we'd checked into the hotel I was on the phone, stitching up a deal for $200,000 with the News of The World in the UK. Next, I arranged an interview with the NBC's *Today Show* in New York.

On the Friday morning I was in on a conference call as Fat Tony did his interview from LA with a News of The World reporter in London. When that finished I was back on the phone tying up arrangements for the *Today Show* interview and checking with the News of The World that all was in hand. With everything done I rushed downstairs to where Vice President Gore was waiting in the Lexus to go to the sold-out luncheon.

'Sorry,' I said as I climbed in the back seat. I was going to tell him about Fat Tony but thought better of it. I didn't tell anyone at the luncheon about him either. I'm not sure that they were a Fat Tony-type crowd.

The luncheon was brilliant and Al Gore was spectacular.

That night was the final function of the tour, an intimate little gathering of 1,400 people at The Peninsula.

I took Vice President Gore to the airport for his flight home on Sunday morning. What I didn't tell him was that I was going to be on a flight to New York a couple of hours later to be at NBC studios when Fat Tony did his interview with Matt Lauer.

As we were driving to Tullamarine Mr Gore rubbed his hand along the upholstery of the Lexus and said, 'This is a great car. I've ordered two of them back home in the States but the waiting list is so long they say I won't get them for a year.'

I told him I'd speak to my contacts at head office in Australia. A month or so later I got word that they had managed to have the two cars delivered to the Gores.

I didn't ask for a commission, but it's nice to know I've got a future as a car salesman if the celebrity speaking and ex-bodyguard market ever drops off.

CHAPTER 5
MR NEW YORK CITY
RUDY GIULIANI (2003)

On 10 September 2001 Rudy Giuliani had no wife, no home and was soon to have no job and no income. Twenty-four hours later, after the worst mass murder ever on US soil, that all changed. In the aftermath of 9/11 Giuliani wasn't just New York's mayor, he was the world's mayor.

The way Giuliani stepped up and led his city, and for that matter his country, in its darkest hour took him from a local identity to a worldwide celebrity. People wanted to meet him, speak to him and listen to what he had to say, and that made him a very admired, and marketable, figure.

When Giuliani and his wife Donna had separated in 2001, she stayed living in Gracie Mansion and he moved into a rented apartment. When they divorced they split their assets and went their separate ways. After 9/11 Mayor Giuliani had no problems getting the best table in the best restaurant in New York City for the rest of his life. It was paying the bills that concerned him.

Like many public servants leaving office after years of high profile but low income, Giuliani decided to go on the personal appearance circuit. He signed a major book deal and joined one of the world's biggest speaking agencies.

After my success with Bill Clinton the previous year, in 2002 I contacted Giuliani's agency and offered him

US$800,000 for eight speaking engagements in Australia and New Zealand. Their answer was a firm no. According to them Giuliani was simply too busy to even consider working internationally.

Never one to take a knock-back lying down, I tried again a couple of times and got the same answer. Too busy, no interest. In fact, they were quite dismissive of the yokel from Down Under.

One day I was talking to my friend and fellow Clinton admirer, Brisbane business leader Sarina Russo, and mentioned that I would love to bring Giuliani to her home town but his agents kept knocking me back.

'Don't worry,' she says. 'I'll make a call.'

Sarina, it turns out, is friends with a woman by the name of Francine LeFrak. Francine is New York royalty. Her father was Samuel J. LeFrak who ran a property development company called the LeFrak Organization. Founded in 1833 by Francine's great-grandfather, Maurice, it was number 45 on Forbes' Top 500 Private Companies. If you've driven through Queens you might have seen a major apartment development that Francine's father built. It's called LeFrak City.

What has all this got to do with Rudy Giuliani? Not a great deal. It's who Francine is married to that is important. His name is Ric Friedberg and he was Mayor Giuliani's director of public relations.

A week after talking to Sarina I'm on holiday in Bali. One of those resorts you go to in order to get away from everyone and everything. The type of place where no one can find you. One morning I'm asleep and the phone next to the bed starts ringing. It's Ric Friedberg. He's found me.

I tell him about my $800,000 offer. He says to stay by the phone and not go anywhere. I'm on an island in the Pacific, where am I going to go?

The next call is from Mike Hess, Giuliani's legal adviser.

'I understand you want to bring Mayor Giuliani to Australia,' he says.

I say I do, but that his speakers agency won't let me.

'Don't worry about them,' he says. 'Mayor Giuliani wants to meet you in New York.'

'When?' I ask, suddenly wide awake.

'Day after tomorrow.'

So much for my vacation. Two days later I'm checking into the Four Seasons Hotel in downtown New York. It's costing a fortune but I figure I have to stay somewhere flash.

As always, I bring a gift. Earlier that year Bill Clinton had told me about a great book he had just read about Winston Churchill by Roy Jenkins. On that recommendation I had read it too and he was right, it was fantastic. As I'm running through the airport I grab a copy for Giuliani. I've also done my research. As part of her legal obligation as a US Senator, Hillary Clinton has to lodge records of her income, and the income of her spouse. It is on the public record so I know that in the previous year Bill Clinton has done 60 speaking engagements at an average of $150,600 each, a total of over $9 million.

At the appointed time Ric Friedberg picks me up at my hotel and we head over to Giuliani's office. When we walk in there must be about nine off-siders there, all interested in what I have to say.

First up I tell Mayor Giuliani about the 10 gigs I have done with President Clinton by this stage, and the part I have played in his successful speaking career and how I would like to do the same for him.

I also present him with the book on Churchill.

'I know this book,' he says, all excited. 'You wouldn't believe it. I read this book during 9/11. I kept thinking, "what would Churchill do now?" He got his people through the Battle of Britain, I had to get my people through 9/11.'

I took the book out of his hands and turned to page 70.

'Mayor Giuliani,' I said. 'When I read this book, I noticed that in 1900 Mark Twain introduced Winston Churchill at a speech he made in New York for which he was paid $100. Mr Mayor, I want to make you a lot more than $100.'

I told him about my plan for eight events in Australia and New Zealand at $100,000 each.

'Can't you do more?' he asked.

I told him my policy was to under-promise and over-deliver. His face lit up.

'Look at this,' he said rifling through a stack of papers on his desk. They were the galleys of his unpublished book, *Leadership*. He pulled out a page with one of the chapter headings on it. 'Under-Promise and Over-Deliver'. Right there and then Rudy Giuliani and I had a rapport. He told me he would have to think about my offer and asked when I would be back in Australia. I said I was heading to the UK first to see my mother.

'Can you get me some work there too?' he asked.

By the time I left New York the next morning I had a signed agreement to represent Mayor Giuliani in any and all territories outside the USA. I felt like saying 'how do you like them apples?' to his speakers agency, but of course I didn't.

I'd like to say that with my help Rudy took the UK by storm. I can't but that doesn't mean I walked away empty-handed. When I got to London I rented an office and hired a bright young lady named Jenny Powell who had done some work for me before in Australia. I bought The Sunday Times Rich List and told her to start ringing. One of the people she got to was the retail magnate Sir Phillip Green, at the time owner of Topshop, Miss Selfridges and British Homes Stores, amongst others. One of the richest men in England, he is also one of the most generous, involved in a number of large charities.

When we asked Sir Phillip if he would like Mayor Giuliani to speak at one of his charity events he wasn't overly interested.

'The one I really want is Henry Kissinger,' he said. 'Can you organise it?'

'Of course,' I said, never one to look a billionaire philanthropist in the mouth.

Sir Phillip got Kissinger, Kissinger got $80,000, and I got my commission.

Fast forward 12 months to 20 May 2003, and for various reasons all plans to bring Rudy Giuliani to Australia are very much on ice. He's had other things to do, I've had other things to do, and he's the furthest thing from my mind. And then the phone next to the bed rings again.

'Max? Ric Friedberg. Mayor Giuliani wants to see you in New York day after tomorrow.'

This time we start getting somewhere. Turns out Rudy is getting married in three days' time. He has more offers for work than he can handle, but he feels the need to get out of the US and see something of the world. He wants to take his new bride, Judith, on a working holiday.

'Max,' he says. 'What can you do for me?'

I offer him $2.2 million for 20 gigs. I'm telling him I'll take him all over Australia and New Zealand and throw in Singapore and Hong Kong for good measure. I've never been to Singapore and Hong Kong, but I haven't got $2.2 million either so I'll go anywhere to find 20 gigs.

To cut a long story short, he doesn't accept my offer. My old friends at Lion Nathan get involved and want to sponsor three functions, in Melbourne, Sydney and Auckland. They employ me to organise the fundraising but once again, just like with the first President Clinton event in Sydney, they don't want me anywhere near Giuliani because, as they see it, I'm a 'brand'. You have to see their point. The boy from Bournemouth is obviously going to detract attention away from the multi-billion-dollar corporation if anyone knows he's involved. Even so, my nose is a little out of joint. I agree to the fundraising but if they want to run Giuliani's schedule, they can have it. I walk away.

When I get a call from Ric Friedberg saying Rudy is keen for me to organise some more gigs, I tell him I'm not interested but he charms me by saying that Giuliani really wants to work with me. Flattered, I tell him I'll put something together in Brisbane, Canberra, Adelaide and Perth. I arrange the Brisbane leg of the tour for the Bank of Queensland and the other three for local charities.

Giuliani's people have only one condition: he wants a private plane. I do some ringing around and get a price on a Lear jet for $91,000, or $13,000 an event for the seven-event tour. With Lion Nathan paying for three trips and me for four, I figure that's no problem and tell Giuliani's people. Actually, it is a problem. A Lear jet is too small. He wants a Gulfstream V (or as they are known in the trade, a G5). I get back on the phone. A G5 is going to cost the best part of $220,000, and that would blow the budget. I start working through my list of the very rich and famous and write to James Packer, Solomon Lew, Crown Casino, Richard Pratt, Rupert Murdoch and John Gandel, hoping they might be able to help me out and donate their G5. One after the other the replies start coming back, and they all start with the same word — 'Sorry'.

Solly's plane is going to be in the south of France, Crown is flying in some high-rollers, the Packers are heading to Argentina. Richard Pratt offers his for the Melbourne to Sydney leg, but that isn't going to be much help.

And then, some great news. Word comes through

that Lachlan Murdoch would like to donate the News Corporation G5 to fly Rudy Giuliani around. Of all the corporate heavyweights in Australia, Lachlan has the most emotional connection to Rudy Giuliani. Lachlan was raised in New York. He went to school there and attended university at Princeton, in neighbouring New Jersey. News Corp's headquarters is in New York City, a few miles from the World Trade Centre. Several News Corp employees were killed in the September 11 attacks.

Lachlan gives us full use of the News Corp jet for the length of Mayor Giuliani's visit — crew, fuel, catering, the works, free of charge.

Giuliani arrives in Sydney on 20 August 2003. Lion Nathan has told me not to be there, but I show up anyway and say g'day. The next night he does a big gig at the Westin Hotel for Lion Nathan. I'm told it went well. I wouldn't know. I wasn't allowed to go.

Friday morning, we hop aboard Lachlan Murdoch's jet and fly to Brisbane for the Bank of Queensland function — an intimate little lunchtime event for 2,100 of Mayor Giuliani's new best friends. On the way Rudy and I start to bond. This is the part of my job I really love. Getting to know people, breaking the ice. I know that Mayor Giuliani is a lover of good wine. I ask if he's ever tried Grange Hermitage. He says he hasn't, so when we arrive in Brisbane I give Sarina Russo a call. She organises with her brother-in-law Gerry Penisi a bottle of Grange for us to have on the flight back to Sydney where the jet drops me off before taking Rudy and his party to Melbourne for the second Lion Nathan event.

A few weeks earlier, Lion Nathan boss (now chairman of Woolworths) Gordon Cairns has rung me to say that they are having problems selling tickets for Sydney and Melbourne. Given that they had told me that they didn't want me involved, I wasn't disposed to help out so all I said was, 'gee Gordon, that's no good'. On the day that Mayor Giuliani was heading to Melbourne he still didn't know whether the event was going ahead. Back in Sydney the next morning I met him at the private plane airbase with a pile of New York Yankee caps to sign. I was wearing my own Yankees cap. As Rudy finished signing the caps I was planning to auction, he took it off my head and signed it as well. I still have it.

I asked him, 'how was Melbourne?'

He said, 'it didn't happen. We sat in our hotel room and watched TV.'

I couldn't believe it. They didn't even take them out to dinner. That's so wrong. Even if it's not for work, you take the talent out and make them feel good.

That day we flew to Canberra for an event at the National Museum. As usual I had my team with me, including Alan Jones who donates his time to MC many of my charity events free of charge, and comedian Brian Doyle. In Canberra we stayed at the Hyatt which is probably my favourite hotel in Australia. It's a beautiful art deco building and as far as Mayor Giuliani was concerned its best feature is its walk-in humidor. A lot of the powerful Americans I have met love cigars. Bill Clinton, Mayor Giuliani, Arnold Schwarzenegger, all love to smoke their 'stogies', and I love the aroma of cigars. My father Leon, who died when I was 15, was a cigar smoker and whenever I smell cigar smoke I always think of him. Mayor Giuliani had a little Tupperware container in which he carried his cigars wherever he went. We spent a pleasant few hours at the Canberra Hyatt, him enjoying smoking his cigars and me thinking about my dad.

Next event on the list was Auckland. Judith had bought a little DVD player with her. They hadn't watched their wedding video yet so they started watching it and invited me to join them. I didn't get to the wedding but I got to watch the video. We were sitting there, with Judith and Rudy pointing out their guests. It was like, 'oh look there's Donald and Melania Trump, there's the Clintons, there's Uncle Salvatore...'

The Auckland show was for Lion Nathan. Again, I'm told it went well. I wouldn't know. I wasn't allowed to go. We then went to Adelaide. The one thing I remember about this event was that when one of the children in the choir fainted, the first two people who rushed to help her were Rudy and Judith.

When in Adelaide we got around a little bit. Rudy, his team and I went shopping at an antique bookshop I know of, owned by Michael Treloar, and bought some old books.

We then flew to Perth for the last of the gigs at Burswood Casino. Judith wasn't keen on the long flight so she went back to Sydney, leaving Rudy, me, Alan Jones, Brian Doyle, a couple of Rudy's advisors and security to make the trip in the Murdoch jet.

Arriving in Perth, Rudy said let's play golf. Next thing, Rudy and I are paired off and playing golf against two of his travelling team, Eric Hatzimemos and Jay Weinkam. Well at least Rudy played golf. I walked around swinging a club and saying 'whoops'. Thanks to Rudy we beat them. After hosting President Clinton and not being able to join him in the course I had invested in some golf lessons. There's a few hundred bucks I'll never get back.

Whenever I hold a function in Perth I always invite Betty Cuthbert. I had also invited cricketer Justin Langer. Before the function started we did a photo-op with Betty, Justin and Rudy. Later that night a few of us head to the casino. By 2am Jonesy is falling asleep in a chair but Rudy and I are still hitting the roulette table. We're up, we're down but eventually I've lost my $400 and a little while later, he has too. By now it's about 4am and Rudy says we should go up to his suite and have breakfast. He's staying in Burswood's enormous Presidential Suite. We catch the lift to his floor and start walking along the corridor. Outside every door is that morning's copy of *The West Australian* newspaper, and there on the front page is the big photo of Rudy with Betty Cuthbert and Justin Langer.

'Look,' he says, 'there's my picture.' He pulls out a pen and signs across the page, 'Best Wishes, Rudy Giuliani'. He then goes along and signs each and every paper along the corridor. It took some time. Mayor Giuliani has a beautiful copperplate signature with swirls and sweeps. He's not a man to be rushed. I just hope the people who picked up their newspapers the next morning thought, 'Oh my gosh, Rudy Giuliani has autographed my copy of *The West Australian*' and not, 'Oh no, some idiot has scribbled all over my morning paper'.

We then had a great breakfast in his room and watched the sun come up before packing for our flight back to Sydney.

After my experience with Bill Clinton and President George Bush Senior, I've become quite used to motorcades, so when I was making arrangements for Giuliani's visit, I reached out to the police wherever he was scheduled to appear and asked would they be able to help out. Because he wasn't a former Head of State, they weren't keen. All except the West Australian police. Because of 9/11 and the way Giuliani had recognised the amazing work of the New York first responders, police departments have great respect for him. In many ways he is regarded as an honorary member of the police community. The WA police did a threat assessment and found that when Giuliani was Attorney General of New York he had made a lot of enemies of organised crime figures. That was good enough for them. They agreed to provide motorcades, and because of that so did the other States.

We all met downstairs in the casino foyer with the motorcade lined up outside on Burswood's long circular driveway. As the luggage was being loaded I told everyone to get in the cars while I went to pay the bill. When I'd settled our account and walked out, the motorcade was gaining speed down the driveway. There we had four or five black limousines, police motorcycles, flashing lights and a lunatic running along behind waving his arms and screaming, 'Stop. Stop. Let me in'.

Thankfully the driver looked in the rear-view mirror and spotted me (and more thankfully the police didn't shoot me) and I got on to the plane. I slept all the way back to Sydney. I know that because Mayor Giuliani took a photo and sent it to me.

As we parted company at Sydney Airport, he and Judith told me that whenever I was in New York I must come and see them and we'd have dinner. A few months later, I did just that and we had a lot of fun. In all my dealings with him, I found him to be a good man; fair, honest and real. The Americans would call him, 'a straight up guy'. I really enjoyed our time together and it was chilling and fascinating to hear him talk about the aftermath of 9/11. He tells a story well, and makes you feel like you are there. I have enormous admiration for him. It is impossible to imagine what he went through at that time. He would attend six, seven, eight funerals a day, consoling, comforting and just being there. I said to him something along the lines of, 'I don't know how you did it' and he said, 'they had elected me as their mayor and it was more important for me to be there for the bad times than for the good'. He was very disciplined, always reliable, always ready to do whatever needed to be done to fulfil his commitments, and also go above and beyond when asked — which is not always the case.

In February 2006 I brought out a number of leading US business people for a seminar, including the former boss of Disney, Michael Eisner and Carly Fiorina, best known for her tenure as CEO of Hewlett Packard and unsuccessful bid for the 2016 Republican Presidential nomination. Eisner was incredible, nothing was too much trouble: photo-ops, interviews, personal appearances, whatever I asked him to do, he would do, always on-time, always without fuss. Carly was different. She followed our agreement to the letter. She would take part in the seminar but nothing else. One day after Michael had given a series of interviews to local media, he asked me if Carly was doing the same. I told him she wouldn't. He shrugged and said, 'if you are going to drink from the well, you have to carry the water.'

Rudy Giuliani is another one who carries the water. To me he is the quintessential New Yorker. He could be the cab driver who picks you up on the corner of West 42nd St and Broadway, the guy sitting next to you at a Yankees game or the one at the newsstand who sells you your morning copy of *The New York Times*.

A couple of years after he had been in Australia, I met Rudy again in the US. He told me he had just done his 500th event. At $100,000 an appearance, that is US$50 million. He has come a long way from that rented apartment in 2001. He now lives in a superb mansion in The Hamptons but I guarantee it hasn't changed him a bit.

To me he will always be Mr New York City.

CHAPTER 6
KEEPING UP WITH THE KARDASHIANS
KIM KARDASHIAN (2010)

The question came from a good contact of mine named Chris Mort who I had met when he worked at the advertising agency owned by my friend John Singleton.

It was 2010 and Chris was now working for McCann Ericson and one of his major clients was Michael Hill, the jeweller.

'Michael wants to give away a $1 million 22 carat diamond,' he said. 'He wants your advice on the best way to do it.'

Well, I told Michael, the first thing is to put it into a ring.

'The second,' I said, 'Is to get Kim Kardashian to promote it.'

I'd like to say that Michael immediately jumped up, put his arms around me and said, 'Max, you're a genius. Why didn't we think of that?'

He didn't. His first reaction was, 'Putting it in a ring could scar the diamond.'

His second was, 'Who's Kim Kardashian? I've never heard of her.'

Obviously, Michael had been too busy becoming a super-successful jewellery retailer to watch a lot of reality TV.

Michael is an incredible success story. Born in New Zealand, his first dream was to become a concert violinist but when he was told he had taken up the instrument too late in life to get to the very top, he began working in the jewellery shop of his uncle. A born salesman and showman, Michael built up the business though innovative advertising and promotional campaigns. Then, at the age of 42 with a wife and two children, his house burned down. He had an epiphany that he needed to own his own jewellery store. When his uncle refused to sell him the business he struck out on his own, with the aim of opening seven stores in seven years. He beat his goal by one store, opening shop number eight a month before the seven-year deadline was up, and moved across the ditch to Australia to further expand his empire.

By the time he asked me to promote the 22-carat diamond campaign, Michael had 70 stores in New Zealand, 200 in Australia, 30 in Canada and nine in Chicago. His company buys and sells over $100 million worth of diamonds every year.

Happily, Michael — or Sir Michael to give him his official title — came around to agreeing with me that offering a $1 million diamond ring as a prize to the contestants judged to be 'The World's Best Couple' sounded a lot more appealing than handing over a huge diamond on its own.

He also did his research and worked out pretty quickly just who Kim Kardashian was.

The original deal that I negotiated was for Kim to do one promotional appearance in New York City in mid-October 2010 to launch the competition, and then another one in December to announce the winner, but once Michael realised how big Kim was he asked, 'can we take her to Toronto and Chicago too?'

I got back on the phone to Kim's people and we arranged to do Monday morning in New York, private plane to Toronto for Monday night and then fly back for Tuesday night in Chicago.

Now you have to realise that organising travel for Kim Kardashian isn't like moving around a former US president like Bill Clinton or George Bush Snr. It's a lot harder than that. Kim has to have people to meet her at the plane and security to get her from the plane to the car. She travels with her own hair and make-up people and a representative from her PR company to jump up and down in case anything goes wrong. Then there is her LA agent who doesn't like to let her out of his sight. I thought President Clinton had an entourage until I travelled with Kim, but I tell you something: I don't begrudge her a thing.

Kim Kardashian is the most professional person I have ever worked with in my life.

Whenever she had to do something, she was there half an hour early, ready to go, and you have to remember: if she was scheduled to be in front of the cameras at 11am she would have been sitting in front of a mirror having her hair and make-up done at 6am. The appearance might only have been for 45 minutes, but the preparation for those 45 minutes was a two-hour operation. Add in the half an hour that she was always early to ensure that she was ready to appear at the allotted time — and I mean always — and you got a lot of Kim Kardashian for your money.

How much money are we talking? Well, for that Michael Hill promotion we paid her US$225,000 for the three gigs, plus we had to fly her and her entourage from LA to New York and back first class and put them up in five-star hotels. Then there were limos, security and a $40,000 private plane for the flights to and from Toronto and Chicago. In the early planning stages, when Michael was baulking at the cost, I even paid $25,000 out of my own fee to make it happen. I couldn't tell you what the final bill was, but I do know this: it would have been cheap at twice the price.

Sometimes in the promotion game you have to give the talent a little nudge from time to time, ask them if they would mind giving the media a little extra. Maybe give a slightly more expansive answer to reporters' questions than 'yep', 'nope' or 'dunno'. Maybe slow down, or even stop, so that photographers can get the shot they need as they walk into a room.

Not with Kim. She knows the game inside out. At all her appearances I would set up the 'media wall' — the photographic backdrop with Michael Hill the Jewellers logos on it. The phalanx of photographers and TV cameras would be fanned out in front of it, each trying to get a clear vantage point. They needn't have worried. Kim was the world's greatest exponent of what is known in the trade as the 'step and repeat'.

Now I admit I didn't know what the 'step and repeat' was until I saw Kim Kardashian in action and, truth be told, it might not even be a real thing, but that's what Kim's handlers call it and that's good enough for me. What she does is start at one side of the wall and look at the photographers immediately in front of her. She will look right into the lens of their camera at exactly the right angle for them to get a perfect front-on shot. She will then take a small step to the side, change her angle slightly and give the exact same pose. Then again and again. Step and repeat, step and repeat, all the way across the wall until every photographer has their picture, as if they and Kim are the only ones in the room.

She is patient, polite, kind and looks immaculate. It really was a pleasure, and an education, to watch her work, but before we started the tour I had a little side-trip to take.

I had arrived in New York a few days early to make sure everything was ready. We had Kim booked into a beautiful hotel, the event was being held at the Rockefeller Center (get it? Rock, as in diamond?), Kim's PR people and I had checked everything out and they had signed off on it all. With Kim's first appearance on Monday 18 October and everything in order, on Saturday the 16th I flew to Rochester to meet with another huge star who I hoped to bring to Australia: Al Pacino.

Rochester, which is in New York State, a 90-minute flight from New York City, was once the bustling headquarters of Kodak. At one stage the company had 60,000 employees living and working in the town, but that was before the digital camera and iPhone brought Kodak — and Rochester — to its knees. By the time I got there in 2010 it wasn't quite a ghost-town, but it was close. The only place showing much sign of life was the campus of the University of

Rochester, which was where Mr Pacino was appearing.

What was Oscar-winner Al Pacino doing on stage at a university more than 4,000km east of Hollywood you ask? Good question. He's an actor and I guess he's always looking for an audience. A couple of years before, he had decided to go onto the celebrity speaking circuit, put together a show and would go wherever his agent booked him.

The show started with a two-minute video showing clips of his most famous movie roles: *The Godfather*, *Dog Day Afternoon*, *Serpico*, *The Scent of a Woman* and others, then the auditorium went black and when the lights came back on there he was, standing on the stage. The place went wild. He got a standing ovation before he even opened his mouth. He then did a Q&A for about 45 minutes followed by some more clips from the two documentaries he directed, *Looking for Richard*, about Shakespeare's *Richard III*, and *Wilde Salome* about Oscar Wilde's staging of the play *Salome*.

The big finish was when he did some readings from *Richard III* and *Salome*. He ended up by reciting Wilde's haunting poem about a hanging that took place when he was behind bars, *The Ballad of Reading Gaol*.

You could have heard a pin drop. The audience was spellbound. I would have loved to bring that show to Australia. It would have been a sensation.

Immediately after the performance Al's agent took me to meet him in his dressing room. I'd once given President Clinton a pair of cufflinks for a gift so I thought I'd give Al a pair as well. He took them out of the box and stuck them in his eyes to be funny. What you might call a sight-gag. It was a bit weird but when Michael Corleone makes a joke, you laugh.

Al had an Australian connection from when he did some ads for Vittoria Coffee. We chatted a bit about Australia and how much he would like to come and I said I'd like to bring him to do some events. I mentioned a figure of $1 million. I hadn't done my sums but for some reason I thought I could get him for $1 million — $900,000 no, but $1 million yes. He said he'd love to perform and if I could work out a deal with his agent, he'd do it.

He then went out into the theatre for a meet and greet and some photographs. I walked out to his car with him and I got to see him interacting with his fans. He was very kind and friendly, waving through the window as he drove off. I thought he was someone I'd really enjoy working with.

Unfortunately, the deal never came off. Every time I spoke to his agent it seemed the price went up an extra $100,000 or $200,000 and in the end I wasn't interested. The offer still stands. He's a superstar.

And speaking of superstars... I flew back to New York City and got ready to jump aboard the Kim Kardashian Express. If I had even the slightest doubt about how big Kim was it was blown away with a phone call first thing Monday morning.

It was Don Walker on the line. Don is Bill Clinton's agent and, as you can imagine, he has rubbed shoulders with some pretty major celebrities in his time. He asked if I could do him a favour.

'My daughter is a huge Kim Kardashian fan,' he said. 'She has never asked me to introduce her to anyone I have ever had anything to do with, but she is desperate to meet Kim. Is there any way you can arrange it?'

I said sure, just bring her along to Rockefeller Center — and getting Don Walker's daughter to meet Kim Kardashian suddenly became the most important job on my list. You have to remember that at this point I still hadn't met Kim myself and you never know how someone is going to behave in that kind of situation but I shouldn't have worried. Kim couldn't have been more gracious. I introduced them, they chatted, she posed for some photos. Don's daughter was completely besotted.

After Don's call I went down to have breakfast in the hotel restaurant with Kim's agent who had flown in from LA. We're just enjoying our coffees when my phone rings. It is Kim's New York-based PR person.

'Where are you?' she says. 'Kim's here at Rockefeller Center and ready to get started.'

I looked at my watch, worried that I had somehow messed up the time zone.

'It's 9.15,' I say. 'She's not on for 45 minutes.'

'That doesn't matter,' she says. 'Kim's ready and she wants to do a walk-through.'

We never did get to finish those coffees. The two of us jumped into a cab, raced the short distance to Rockefeller Center and, sure enough, there was Kim, looking a million dollars and ready to go.

And so were the photographers and TV cameras. They were

everywhere, staking their claim for a bit of ground in front of the media wall. I compered the event, and introduced Michael Hill who gave a short speech about the quality of the diamond and how pleased he was to be able to make it available to some lucky couple.

From memory my introduction and Michael's speech went something like this, 'Blah, blah, blah, blah, diamond. Blah, blah, blah, blah, Kim Kardashian.'

That's what the media and guests heard anyway. No one was really interested in anything we had to say. All they wanted was a picture of Kim, and we gave them the money shot — Michael slipping the ring on Kim's finger. As he did, the camera drives were all making clickety, clickety, clickety noises with the flashes going off like strobe lights at a nightclub. It was a Princess Diana-type media frenzy, which just confirmed that Kim really was reality TV royalty.

The photos went around the world and Michael couldn't have been happier.

We had booked Kim into a suite at one of New York's best hotels at $4,000 for the night, but as it turned out we could have saved our money. Better still, I could have used the suite myself because Kim didn't need it. She spent the night in New Jersey with the basketballer Kris Humphries, who she would marry (and divorce) the next year.

Later that day we got on the private plane and headed to Toronto where we went through the same thing again. Other than the fact that this time it was an evening function, it could have been identical — right down to the phone call from the PR lady.

'Where are you? Kim is here and we're sitting in the car outside.'

I had to ask her to tell the driver to go around the block a few times and come back in 15 minutes.

As always, Kim was brilliant. She did the step and repeat, looked great, Michael took the diamond out of its beautiful box, slipped it on her finger, the cameras went clickety, clickety, click and it got blanket coverage.

Afterwards I had arranged for part of the function room to be set aside so we could relax and catch our breath. For the first time it gave me an opportunity to sit down and have a chat with Kim and get to know her a little better. This was October and she told me about some of her plans for the next year which included four reality TV shows. She had *Keeping Up with the Kardashians*, there was one that she was doing with her sister, *Kourtney and Kim Take New York*, another that she was involved in with a friend and one other. Then there were product endorsements and personal appearances that she could list, date and time. This wasn't someone who was just being told where to be at what time and showing up. She was very much in control of her life and her career. This was one seriously together lady.

From Toronto we headed on to the last stop on the Kim Kardashian roadshow, an invitation-only function at one of Michael's stores in Chicago. When we arrived at the airport at the appointed time to hop aboard the private plane, there sitting on the tarmac in her limo was Kim. She'd been there half an hour early, of course.

The Chicago gig the next night went as smoothly as all the others, but it held special significance for me. Growing up around my father's aquashow in Bournemouth I would hear all the great old show tunes every night. For some British kids in the '60s the music of bands like The Beatles, Rolling Stones and Gerry and the Pacemakers was the soundtrack of their youth. Not me. As an eight or nine-year-old I was more likely to be walking around whistling something from *Showboat* or *South Pacific* that dad had incorporated into one of his extravaganzas.

So, that night at the Michael Hill store in some shopping mall in downtown Chicago, finding myself with a captive audience and a microphone in my hand, I couldn't resist.

'Ladies and gentlemen,' I said. 'Michael Hill and Kim Kardashian will be here in a moment, but first, a song...'

At which point I launched into, *'Chicago, Chicago, that toddlin' town. Chicago, Chicago, I'll show you around...'*

I'd like to say the 200 in attendance joined in, clapping and singing, totally won over by my infectious salute to their hometown, but I can't. I think they were more confused than touched, but I didn't care. Dad would have loved it.

I really enjoyed my first visit to Chicago and, according to the gossip columnists, Kim had a good time there too. After the function she was spotted out on the town with Kanye West whom she married following her divorce from Kris Humphries.

After Chicago, Kim and the Glam Squad flew out of my life until we got back together in December for the naming of the winner of the $1 million diamond ring. Open to couples living in the US, Canada, New Zealand and Australia, where Michael Hill has stores, it wasn't just a case of them filling in a form and waiting to be drawn out of the barrel. It was an online contest involving 16 different challenges, ranging from submitting favourite photos, revealing their pet names for each other and making a video showing public displays of affection. In the three months or so that the competition ran, thanks in no small part to Kim's involvement, it received over 350,000 entries. With all of Michael's US stores in Chicago, much of the promotional work leading up to the judging had been done there, with 'the ring' (actually a cubic zirconium copy with the real one safely locked away in a bank vault) on show in the shop windows. Another ring had also gone on the road through Canada and to LA, Auckland and Sydney. We also took it to the Melbourne Cup where it was shown off live on television from one of the corporate marquees. The official Melbourne Cup jeweller, Hardy Brothers, was not impressed.

While this was all going on the members of the judging panel were sifting through the hundreds of thousands of entries. Head judge was Sir Michael, of course, along with Candace Bushnell, the former New York newspaper columnist best known for writing *Sex in The City*, and Kathryn Eisman, the LA-based Australian fashion writer who authored the two best-sellers *How to Tell a Woman by her Handbag* and *How to Tell a Man by his Shoes*. I also received a phone call from a Chicago PR woman who asked if her client Jeanine Pirro could be a judge. Actually,

Jeanine Pirro is a judge. A real one. Or she was anyway. Now she is a TV judge, with her show *Justice with Judge Jeanine* a ratings-winner on Fox.

'How much will she cost us?' I asked.

'Nothing,' she said.

It suddenly struck me that Jeanine Pirro was just who we were looking for, and I added her to the panel.

The winners were Cameron and Shariyah Morris who lived in Auckland. Cameron was a Kiwi and Shariyah was originally from Seattle, Washington. We flew them to New York for the announcement on 14 December at Lavo Nightclub on 57th Street. Cameron and Shariyah were a fantastic young couple and the ring looked incredible, but once again it was Kim who stole the show. She walked in, the paparazzi went crazy, she did the step and repeat, smiled, hugged Michael, hugged Cameron and Shariyah, smiled some more, did a couple more step and repeats and floated out of the room and, sadly, out of my life.

Or should I say, out of my league.

It had only been a few months since I had last seen Kim but a lot had happened to her in that short space of time. Does the date 6 October 2010 mean anything to you? Probably not, but the Kardashian family has many millions of reasons to remember it. That was the day that Instagram was launched; the day the game changed; the day that Kim Kardashian and her family were given a money-printing machine.

Remember I said that in October 2010 I secured the services of Kim for three gigs at US$75,000 each? A year later I wouldn't have got her for three times that — all because of Instagram.

How do I know this? Well, in 2017 I tried to do a deal with Kim's half-sister Kylie Jenner to do a one-hour appearance and one Instagram post. I started by offering US$100,000 and I didn't even get a reply. I kept upping my offer until finally they told me that Kylie would do it for half a million dollars US. I thought they were just testing me so I said, ok, I'll give her $350,000. Turns out they weren't testing me at all. They were totally serious. No, they said, she won't do it. I asked, why not?

You know that expression, 'I wouldn't get out of bed for less than...'? Well, I can tell you how much it takes to get Kylie Jenner out of bed. According to her agents, it's $150,000.

'She can just sit on her bed at home and get paid $150,000 for one post on Instagram,' they told me.

To make that sort of money all Kylie — and the rest of her family — has to do is take a selfie of themselves showing off their new watch and post it on Instagram with a comment like, 'Isn't my new watch beautiful? It's a Cartier. You should get one too.'

You have to realise that when the Kardashians get behind something, it generates tens of millions of dollars' worth of sales. Obviously, any company is going to pay big money to have that sort of selling power, and these days they probably take a piece of the back end as well. Since the explosion of Instagram, the Kardashians now have their own make-up and jewellery lines. They pre-promote their products. They say 'get your orders in now, only 10 days to go, only five days'. They sell out on the first day and they then take all those posts off so the Instagram feed looks clean until the next offer.

It's a well-oiled machine and the best part as far as promoters are concerned is that when you get one Kardashian, you get the lot — and their army of followers.

It's some army. If you look up the Top 20 most followed people on Instagram five of them are Kardashians. Number five, with around 118 million followers is Kim, followed by Kylie, Kendall, Khloe and Kourtney. Selena Gomez might be number one, with around 143 million, but if you add up all the Kardashians in the Top 20 you are accessing almost half a billion followers, and that's not even factoring in Kris, Caitlin and all the others, nor their enormous Facebook and Twitter followings, taking their reach to over a billion followers.

All of which explains why I'll probably never work with Kim again, which is a great shame. I would love to. She is everything I look for in a celebrity. She is a guaranteed magnet for the media; she always does what she says she is going to do; she is fun to be around, and she is always half an hour early.

As a matter of fact, there is only one thing that I don't like about Kim Kardashian.

I can't afford her.

CHAPTER 7
THE BLAIR RICH PROJECT
TONY BLAIR (2011)

Tony Blair left office in 2007 and I immediately reached out to his people and said what I always say to politicians who have just entered the real world after years of public service and low salaries. 'I'd like to make you rich'. I started off by offering a speaking tour for a small seven figure sum. I waited and waited throughout the rest of the year hoping for a reply that never came. In 2008 I followed up and played the waiting game for another fruitless 12 months. In 2009 I tried again and finally in 2010 I contacted the agent and said I was withdrawing my offer.

I wasn't too concerned because I had an ace up my sleeve — a signed contract to bring Arnold Schwarzenegger to Australia in February 2011. In November I told Arnie's agent I was going to announce the tour and start selling tickets. She got straight back to me and said, 'You can't do that. He's still Governor of California. He can't be advertising any financial dealings while he's in office.'

I asked when I could announce the tour. They told me January. That would give me six weeks to sell tickets, get all the money in, finalise arrangements and have everything ready to go. It was simply impossible, so I had to terminate the deal.

It's a funny thing in my game. When one door closes another often opens and out of the blue the phone was ringing and Tony Blair's agent, who I couldn't get to talk to me for three years, was suddenly my best friend.

Tony had a hole in his very full calendar and his agent was wondering if my offer could be put back on the table. It sure could, and we did a deal for him to come in July 2011. One thing you soon learn about Tony Blair, he's a very hard worker. We arranged a two-country tour with seven events in five cities over four days.

Anthony Pratt agreed to sponsor the tour, and just as importantly he agreed to provide his magnificent Bombardier Global Express jet. We never could have even considered that full-on schedule without it.

Tony and Cherie Blair flew into Melbourne on Monday 25 July and hardly stopped to draw breath for the next five days. The morning after they arrived, Tony did a press conference with Prime Minister Julia Gillard and the next day we had a lunch for 600 people at the Sofitel Hotel before a dinner for 60 at Anthony's family home and mansion *Raheen*.

The next morning we flew to Auckland for a lunch for 500. The function was at Eden Park, the home of rugby union and we felt like we'd been caught on the bottom of a ruck by the time we got in there. There were serious protests all around the ground with people chanting and holding up signs calling Tony a warmonger and murderer for his involvement in the Gulf War. Luckily, we had good security in the shape of a detachment of officers from

Scotland Yard, sent and paid for by the British government. Having now seen them both in action I'm not sure who I would less like to upset, Scotland Yard or the US Secret Service. Let's call it a tie.

That night there was a dinner function in Brisbane for 700, and the next morning we flew to Sydney for a lunch. We barely had time to finish dessert before we were back at the airport catching the plane across the country to Perth where we had another dinner for 600.

The next morning, we flew from Perth to Sydney. Needless to say, it had been an incredibly tight schedule with no time for anything like the golf and shopping that President Clinton enjoyed on his visits. Mr Blair might have been a former prime minister but he was also working as a United Nations Middle East peace envoy. When he arrived in Australia he had just completed his 68th visit to the region and when he wasn't speaking at functions or asleep he was always on the phone dealing with matters in the Middle East. He would talk to both sides at least five times a day. At the time there were two crucial issues that he was involved with. The first was what was known as the Gaza Strip Cottage Cheese Crisis. Cottage cheese is the cornerstone of breakfast in Israeli homes and is therefore important spiritually as well as tasting good. When some Israelis discovered that they were paying a lot more for their cottage cheese than people in the US and Europe, they took to Facebook to protest. Before long the Gaza Strip was in uproar, and it threatened the stability of the region. I can tell you from first-hand knowledge that Tony Blair spent a lot of time discussing the price of cottage cheese in July 2011. The other matter he was involved in was the cost of housing which was considered almost as important as the cost of cheese at that time.

Tony is an incredibly bright and personable man with a truly magnetic personality. He also has a genuine love for Australia and told me he would love to come here more often and could even see himself living here. Even so, the only time I saw Tony really letting his hair down and relaxing on that trip was on the flight from Perth back to Sydney. Coming along for the ride was the former premier of Western Australia Geoff Gallop who, it turned out, was Tony's best mate at Oxford University. The entire trip they sat together telling stories about the old days and laughing about their exploits like naughty schoolboys. It was great to see.

What a lot of people don't know about Tony Blair is that before he became one of the world's most powerful politicians, he had dreams of becoming a music and theatre promoter. His first year out of high school was spent in London trying to break into show business. When he failed to discover the next Beatles or Spice Girls he enrolled at Oxford, but he didn't lose his theatrical ambitions. Apparently, he and Geoff Gallop spent as much time putting on shows at the university as they did studying. Geoff had us in stitches talking about the time Tony talked him into going on stage wearing nothing but a jockstrap and a dressing gown and doing an ad-lib impression of a typical Australian. If typical Australians wore nothing but jockstraps and dressing gowns, that is.

At that time the Australian newspapers were full of stories about the recently released archived letters of our longest serving prime minister, Sir Robert Menzies. I asked Tony who Great Britain's longest serving prime ministers had been. He reeled them off like he was on a quiz show, 'Walpole, Liverpool, Maggie Thatcher.'

That got us talking about the longest serving world leaders.

'Your mate Gaddafi is number one,' Geoff said to Tony.

I asked about Fidel Castro and Geoff said Castro had actually resigned at one stage and come back, so he didn't count but it did prompt Tony to tell a Castro anecdote.

'I was at a conference in Geneva and this tall bearded man tapped me on the shoulder,' he said. 'When I turned around he started berating me in Spanish. I don't speak Spanish but the Brazilian delegate was there trying to translate. Then it suddenly dawned on me who the big man with the beard was — Fidel Castro. I just went, Fidel Castro. Cool. Can I have your autograph?' I don't think he got the autograph, but it did diffuse the situation.

That night we had a dinner for 40 people at Anthony Pratt's spectacular apartment overlooking Sydney Harbour. I remember that function particularly well because I was sitting next to future Australian Prime Minister Malcolm Turnbull. It was at the time that Twitter was just taking off and rather than talk to each other Mr Turnbull and I decided it was much more fun to converse via Twitter. Well, it seemed like fun at the time anyway. That was a great night. Whether it had something to do with the time he had spent with his old mate Geoff Gallop I don't know, but

Tony was in fine form. The dinner started with Brian Doyle doing his comedy routine. One of the jokes he told was about when he was young and wild and playing up every night. Finally, his father said to him, 'Brian don't you think it's time you found a girl who enjoys doing all the things you like doing and settled down?' To which he answers, 'Where am I going to find a drunken lesbian?' The story continues, 'the next thing you know you're walking down the aisle. Your family on one side, and on the other, the Planet of the Apes.'

When Tony got up to speak, the first thing he said was, 'Brian, I didn't know you were at my wedding.' Cherie's head shot up and the look she gave him was priceless.

Tony is a fantastic speaker. I put him right up with President Clinton as one of the best speechmakers in the world. In fact, I told Cherie during that trip that I rated Tony the best speaker I had ever heard. She said, 'what about President Clinton?' As I said to her, the difference between them is the way they use humour in their speeches. President Clinton has a good sense of humour too, but he might slip a funny little line in here and there to relax the crowd. Tony Blair is different. He intersperses his funny stories with the serious subjects he wants to cover. His anecdotes aren't just an add-on to the speech, they are very much part of it. And the man is seriously funny. Some speakers might get a polite little chuckle from the audience. Tony combines the gravity of a world leader with the timing and delivery of a comedian and he gets belly laughs.

Most of Tony's humour revolves around genuine

anecdotes about his time in office. Others are plain old-fashioned jokes, usually with a political angle like the one he tells about the politician who dies and goes up to the Pearly Gates.

'Heaven or Hell?' asks St Peter. The politician says he doesn't want to rush into anything and would like to weigh up his options.

'Sure,' says St Peter and opens the gate to Heaven. The politician looks around and it's very nice, calm, serene — and a little boring.

So St Peter sends him to Hell where the Devil greets him and it looks sensational. There's great music, beautiful people sipping drinks with little umbrellas in them, sexy women walking around and 24-hour partying.

He goes back to St Peter and says, as much as he likes Heaven, it looks a lot more fun in Hell, so he'd like to go there. St Peter sends him down where the Devil opens the door and it's horrible. It's filthy dirty, raining, dank and smelly. People are moaning and crying.

The politician looks at the Devil and says, 'What's happened? This isn't what it looked like last time.'

'Oh,' says the Devil. 'We were campaigning then.'

I probably can't do justice to the anecdotes he tells, because a lot of it is in the way he puts them across, but I'll try my best. One he tells is about the first time he met the Queen. When he became prime minister, he had to go to the palace for his first audience with Her Royal Highness. Before the meeting he had to wait outside and was instructed by one of the Queen's staff about the correct protocol. He was told to stand outside the door until told to go in, then to take two steps towards Her Majesty and bow. Under no circumstances he was told, was he to touch the Queen.

'So,' he says, 'I waited until I was told to enter, walked in, tripped over a little step and fell right on top of her. That was my first meeting with the Queen.'

He never said if things improved.

Another behind-the-scenes insight he gave us was a story about when the movie *The Queen*, portraying their relationship in the days after the death of Princess Diana, was released.

'She said to me, "I believe they have made a movie about us". I said, "Yes Ma'am". She said, "I'm not going to see it. Are you?" I said, "No Ma'am".'

And he never has.

He says when he was prime minister he never had a mobile phone which, given all the phone hacking drama that was hitting the headlines at the time of his visit, probably wasn't such a bad thing. Even so, the day after he left office he bought a mobile and sent his first-ever text message.

'Being new to it I didn't realise the message wouldn't

include my name. A few seconds after sending it I got a reply which asked, "Who is this?" All I could think was, "it's only been 24 hours and they've forgotten me already".'

Now anyone who knows me knows that I love a good joke. I love hearing them, and I love telling them, so when Tony told a story that reminded me of one of my favourite jokes I couldn't help but tell it to him.

Tony's story went like this:

'In 2000 my son Leo was born, making him the first baby to be born at Number 10 Downing St for 152 years, so I don't know what my predecessors were doing while they were in office. In the months leading up to Leo's birth I was engaged in the Irish peace talks, having weekly meetings with the various parties. One day one of the Irish delegates asked me what our new son was going to be named. I told him "Leo, after my father". A few weeks after Leo's birth I noticed that same delegate had a very nice sun tan. "You're looking very tanned," I told him. He said. "I owe it all to you." I asked him what he meant and he said, "Well sir, when you told me what you were naming the lad I popped straight around to the betting shop and put a hundred pounds on the name Leo at ten to one. That thousand pounds paid for a very nice holiday in Spain."'

When Tony told that story at the first lunch in Melbourne I couldn't help but tell him my joke.

It starts with an Australian, an Englishman and an Irishman going on a trip to Europe together and visiting Rome. They're on a tour of the Vatican and the tour guide tells them not to leave the group, but they can't help themselves and wander down a corridor and open a door into a big room. There lying on a table is the body of the Pope. A priest comes bursting into the room and says, 'Gentlemen, gentlemen, you're not supposed to be here. No one must know that the Pope is dead until we have informed all the Cardinals and Archbishops. You must promise me that you won't tell anyone what you have seen until the end of next week.' They promise and re-join the tour party but afterwards the Australian gets them together and says, 'Listen fellas. We've got to keep our promise but there's no harm in us making a buck out of this. We can place bets that the Pope is going to die next week and clean up.'

At the end of the next week the Pope's death is announced and the three of them meet up in a pub in London. The Englishman asks the Australian how he fared. 'Bloody great,' says the Aussie, 'I put a hundred quid on at 100 to one and collected 10,000 quid. How about you?'

The Englishman says he did even better. 'I put 200 quid on at 150 to one for a 30,000 return.'

They turn to the Irishman and ask, 'And how did you go, Paddy?'

'Not so good,' he says. 'I took him in a double with the Archbishop of Canterbury.'

Boom-boom. I told Tony he could use it if he ever got desperate.

But much as Tony's jokes were great and I thought mine was just as good, neither of us got the biggest laugh of the tour. That distinction goes to former Australian prime minister Bob Hawke.

It was at the Friday lunch in Sydney. There were about 600 people at the Darling Harbour Convention and Entertainment Centre. Tony had asked me specifically to invite Bob and sit him at the main table because he had been a huge admirer of his when he was Australian PM and Tony was just making his way up in the British Labour Party. Also on that table were Tony and Cherie, Anthony Pratt, Sarina Russo, who is a close friend of Cherie, Carla Zampatti and someone else whose name I don't know.

What I do know is that he was sitting in my seat. What happened was, I had met this person somewhere and, as I do to dozens of people as I move around the country, I'd said, 'Oh, you must come along to my next function as my guest.' So, sure enough, they rock up to Darling Harbour and tell one of the staff, 'I'm Max Markson's guest'. The staff member looks at the table list, sees my name next to Table 1 and leads them over. By the time I get there after overseeing the pre-lunch rigmarole and photo line every seat on the table is gone — including mine, which has gone to this blow-in who is currently regaling Tony Blair and Bob Hawke with his life story. Not wanting to make a scene or embarrass the guy, whoever he is, I find a chair at the back of the room.

Bob was 81 at the time but still looking fit and tanned and with a twinkle in his eye.

When Tony got up to speak, the opening of his talk was pretty much a tribute to Bob.

'Future Prime Minister Gordon Brown and I used to sit at his feet in 1982 when I was a nobody,' he said.

He then looked down at Bob and said, 'Bob, what is your secret. How do you manage to look so good?'

In a voice that could be heard at the back of the room (I know this because I was at the back of the room and I heard it) Bob shouted back, 'Sex'.

There aren't too many people in the world who can upstage Tony Blair when he is in front of a microphone, but Bob Hawke did that day.

Two days later I waved Tony and Cherie off at Sydney Airport. Sarina Russo tells me that every time she visits them in London they tell her to tell me they want to come back.

We haven't managed to arrange it yet but I'm looking forward to it. Tony will have some great new stories by then.

CHAPTER 8
I LIKE MIKE
MIKE TYSON (2012)

Mike Tyson is the baddest man on the planet, right? Someone you wouldn't want to meet on a dark night or let play with your kids, right?

Wrong. Mike Tyson is a pussycat. A big, sweet guy with a lovely sense of humour.

The Mike Tyson I spent time with is anyway.

The other Mike Tyson? The one we used to see knocking out the world's best heavyweights as if they were cardboard cut-outs; the one who wrote the most shocking stories of crime and drug abuse in his autobiography; the one with a record as long as your arm?

Well, I never saw that Mike Tyson. Thank goodness.

My experience with Mike Tyson started early in 2012 when I found myself at a big event in Melbourne featuring Ben Johnson, the disgraced Canadian sprinter who was disqualified for drug use after winning gold in the 100m at the Seoul Olympics.

I ended up having breakfast with the guy who had brought Ben out. He was also mates with Maradona and we were talking about whether bringing the soccer great to Australia would be possible, amongst other things.

'You know who you should bring out?' he said. 'Mike Tyson. He's doing a show in Las Vegas and I hear it's great.'

Actually, it was more than great. It was a sensation, and Mike wasn't just doing Vegas, he'd also done his Spike Lee-produced show, *Mike Tyson: Undisputed Truth* to packed houses on Broadway.

Now as it happened, the previous year when I was up to my eyeballs arranging Tony Blair's tour of Australia, I received a phone call from a promoter in England. He told me he had done 40 or 50 gigs with Mike Tyson and would I like to bring him to Australia? I said that I was far too busy with Tony Blair to even think about Tyson, but thanks anyway. That night, after the breakfast meeting had piqued my interest, I found the Englishman's number and gave him a call.

'Remember me?' I said. 'About Mike Tyson...' By the time I went back down to breakfast the next morning the deal was done to bring Mike to Australia and New Zealand for six shows over six days.

All I needed was to get him a visa.

When I say 'all I needed was to get him a visa', what I should have said was 'all I needed was to walk backwards and barefoot up Mt Everest'. It was that easy.

Obviously the Australian and New Zealand visa people had never met the nice, friendly Mike Tyson that I got to know. Unfortunately, I think they had read his book. They certainly had a copy of his criminal record, which included a jail term for rape.

So, I hire Chris Carman, a visa expert in Sydney, and he starts the process. We fill in a pile of forms, get references, send off for FBI and US police reports. It is a major, major deal, but ever the optimist I'm confident it will all be sorted and push ahead.

The visa process takes up most of June and July and in August I announce that Mike will be coming Down Under in November. I head over to Las Vegas and organise a video media conference with journalists in all the places Mike will be appearing — Perth, Adelaide, Melbourne, Sydney, Brisbane and Auckland.

It will be the first time Mike has ever been to Australia or New Zealand and the publicity we get is enormous.

There's just one question that all the journalists ask that is a little bit of a worry.

'What about a visa?' they say.

'Oh that. It'll all be fine,' I reply, my fingers firmly crossed behind my back.

One person who doesn't help matters is Melbourne media heavyweight Neil Mitchell who comes out with a damning editorial saying that Mike Tyson is not the sort of person we want in our country and that under no circumstances should the Australian government grant him a visa.

I ask for the right of reply and Neil very kindly agrees to a friendly debate about the issue on his radio show.

Friendly debate is one way to describe it. Stand up stoush is another.

I tell Neil that Mike Tyson has paid the price for his actions and is now an exemplary citizen just trying to put food on the table. The way Neil has been talking you'd think Mike is some sort of animal who is going to run amok and endanger the health and morals of Australian youth and womanhood. I tell the facts, that he's a quiet-living middle-aged family man who will be bringing his wife, two children and mother-in-law with him to Australia, and rather than doing harm to our country and its citizens he'll be providing enormous financial benefit through the hire of venues and the travel and accommodation needs of his many fans.

I think I went pretty well if I do say so myself. It might not have been a knockout win of Tysonesque proportion but I'm confident most judges would have scored it a clear points decision to me.

We start selling tickets. The New Zealand event is at the Vecta Arena (now Spark Arena) in Auckland. With its big Islander population boxing is huge in New Zealand. Especially heavyweight boxing, with a match-up between hard-hitting Samoan-Kiwi David Tua and Mike Tyson talked about for years. The closest 'The Tuamanator' got to the belt was when he lost to Lennox Lewis in 2000, but given their similar fighting styles Tua and Tyson remain legendary figures in New Zealand boxing circles and when it is announced that 'Iron Mike' will be coming to town the demand for seats goes through the roof. Things are looking great, and they look even better when the Kiwi immigration authorities give Mike's visa the green light.

'How good is this?' I think.

Within 24 hours the New Zealand Prime Minister John Key over-rules the decision.

'How bad is this?' I think.

To keep with the boxing analogies, the problem with the

New Zealand PM giving Mike an uppercut is that it has the potential to be a one-two knockout punch. The press jumps on the story and the controversy begins: if New Zealand won't let Mike Tyson into the country, why should Australia?

Happily, the Australian authorities aren't influenced by what our cousins over the Tasman think and the visa is granted: Mike Tyson is coming.

Mike arrives at Sydney airport with his wife Kiki, daughter Milan, son Morocco and Kiki's mother Rita, on Thursday 15 November 2012.

They had flown commercial from the US and had to walk from the international terminal over to domestic to catch a Virgin flight to Brisbane.

I've seen some pretty amazing reactions in my time, but the looks on the faces of the people at Sydney Airport seeing Mike Tyson walking past takes the cake. I should have taken a picture and sent it to the Oxford Dictionary. They could have used it for the definition of 'gobsmacked'.

We went into the Virgin lounge and Mike picked up a copy of *The Australian* newspaper and started reading a story about Aboriginal cave art. I hadn't spoken to Mike at length before but he wanted to discuss the article, and the history of Aboriginal art, in depth. And when I say in depth, I mean in depth. Aboriginal art isn't one of my pet subjects, but I did my best. It didn't take me long to realise that Mike is a very thoughtful and intelligent man.

We all boarded the plane together and settled down for the flight. At the time the hottest book on the best-seller list was *Fifty Shades of Grey*. It wasn't necessarily something you would read in public but as we were in the middle of the flight I noticed a copy lying on the floor. I picked it up and said, 'has somebody lost this?'

'It's mine,' Kiki said sweetly, and popped it back into her travel bag.

We checked into the Stamford Heritage, a beautiful hotel on the Brisbane River next to the Botanical Gardens. Just me and Mike and his family. Oh, and his agent from the UK, his UK security detail and my own security people.

I asked Mike if there was anything he needed.

'A PlayStation and some games,' he said.

I called down to reception and the hotel sent someone out to buy them and charged the cost to the room. A maintenance man connected it all up and handed Mike the controls and for the next week, apart from two occasions, Mike never had those controls out of his hands. If he wasn't doing scheduled appearances or sleeping or eating, he was playing PlayStation.

The funny thing was, when the tour was over I asked him if he had enjoyed himself.

'I've had the best time of my life,' he told me.

'But Mike, you didn't do anything,' I said.

'I know,' he said. 'But that was a really good PlayStation.'

That first afternoon we had a media conference at the back of the hotel, overlooking the river. To give all the TV cameras and newspaper editors a good picture opportunity (or photo-op as it's known in the trade) I had arranged to have a koala there for Mike to hold.

I could just see it: pictures of Mike Tyson cuddling a

koala bear on every newspaper, website and TV channel in the world.

As we walked out onto the hotel patio the handler brought the cute little animal towards us.

'There you go Mike,' I said. 'Just hold the koala for the cameras.'

He literally jumped.

'Hold that thing?' he squealed. 'Are you crazy? No way.'

It was no act. Big Bad Iron Mike was scared out of his wits. So much for the photo-op.

In the days leading up to the media conference I had received dozens of calls from reporters asking for one-on-one interviews with Mike. One who was especially insistent was Nova breakfast radio host Ash Bradman who is a huge Tyson fan. I told Ash what I have to tell everyone in those cases. Sorry, I can't make any promises. Just come along, see how Mike feels and after the all-in if he wants to talk to you, he will.

Ash and his two co-hosts David 'Luttsy' Lutterall and Kip Wightman turned up with their recording gear and high hopes. Unfortunately they, and everyone else, had those hopes scuppered by a young lady from one of the local TV stations.

She had obviously been told by her producer to get Mike to react angrily to her questioning in order to get some footage of him doing his block on the evening news.

Her question went something like this: 'Mr Tyson why should any Queensland woman go along to see you when you have served time in jail for rape?'

Mike answered very civilly.

'They don't have to do anything. If they want to come they can come. If they don't want to come they don't have to.'

She had another crack at it and got the same answer.

When she had a third go he said, 'I already answered that' and headed back inside, with Ash, Luttsy and Kip hot on his trail.

'Mike, Mike, Ash Bradnam from Nova breakfast... Mike, Mike... I'm Ash Bradnam. I'm your biggest fan,' Ash called forlornly, holding his microphone towards Mike's fast disappearing back.

Finally, with Mike safely inside and headed back to his room, Ash just stood there looking totally deflated, as Luttsy and Kip laughed themselves silly.

I suppose you're wondering if Mike went berserk and tore the room apart when he got upstairs. Actually no. He was fine. He played a bit of PlayStation and then we went out for a signing session.

When I was first negotiating the deal with Mike's UK agent I asked him, 'Will Mike sign autographs?'

He answered: 'He laps it up like a dog to a bowl of water.'

If you want to know how Mike Tyson makes a living these days, this is it. He signs his name and has his photo taken. We had arranged a signing session in the middle of the Brisbane CBD and when we arrived the line looked like it stretched halfway to Sydney.

We had settled on a price scale of $100 a signature and $300 a photo, with proceeds split fifty-fifty. Big mistake.

We should have charged twice as much. It's crazy how popular he is.

He's good at it too. He has a great sense of the theatrical. If someone asks for a picture of Mike biting his ear, he'll do it — and do it well. I've got one myself. He gives time to people, shakes their hand when he signs an autograph, makes them feel special.

It's an amazing thing. Imagine being paid to sign your name. It's well known that Mike made and lost around $250 million from boxing, but he and his family will never go hungry because people will always want a piece of paper with his name on it, or a photo of him pretending to punch them on the chin.

He might have lost his world title to Evander Holyfield in November 1996, but Mike Tyson is still one of the most famous people in the world, and he'll never go out of fashion.

When it came time for Mike to do his first show I asked his agent what special requirements he had.

'A microphone,' he said.

'That's it?' I asked.

'That's it,' he said.

I asked about someone to introduce him or interview him on stage.

'Doesn't need it,' he said. 'You can do it.'

'But what do I say?' I asked.

'Just ask him to tell you about his life,' he said.

So that's what I did. Mike walked on to the stage and I said, 'So Mike, tell us about your life…'

And that was it.

He started by saying, 'My mother was a prostitute, my father was a pimp and I was arrested thirty times before I was 12 years old,' and for the next hour he didn't stop talking.

He is so funny; as good as any stand-up. He's very physical. He bounces around the stage like he's still in the ring. Sweats like it too. He shadow punches and waves his arms around, and his stories range from very poignant to downright hilarious.

He says anything that he wants to say. He's very honest and he's not afraid of anyone — he is Mike Tyson after all — and when it comes to name-dropping Mike is up there with the best.

One story he told was about when he was having problems with his first wife Robin Givens. He goes round to her house and is knocking on the door but no one answers. He keeps knocking. The longer he knocks, the angrier he gets — and then he sees a car pulling up with two people in it: Robin Givens and a man. He runs over and is about to drag the man out of the car and make like he's a punching bag, when he recognises him

'It's Brad Pitt,' he says. 'I can't hit him. It's Brad Pitt. I love Brad Pitt...'

He told some beautiful stories about his first trainer and father-figure Gus D'Amato, and some not so beautiful stories about when he hit rock bottom and sunk into a mire of drug abuse and bad company. One of the stories from that period was about a fight he had outside a nightclub.

'I kicked that guy so hard,' he said looking upwards, 'that I saw him going to the moon.'

Every show was different. No one knew beforehand what Mike was going to say, and that included Mike, but everything he said was brilliant, and the crowds loved it.

After the main part of the show we would have a Q&A session with the audience. In the auditorium at the Perth Arena some guy waiting to ask a question got so excited to be near Mike Tyson that he fell four metres off the stage into the orchestra pit.

As well as the shows and the signing sessions we did some private dinners for up to $3,000 a head. In Melbourne at an after show round-table dinner for 20 organised by Mick Gatto I found myself talking to a man named Sean Buckley. Sean told me he ran a company called Ultra Tune and he needed some help with promotions and advertising.

'Ultra Tune,' I said. 'What do you do?'

He told me they tuned cars.

'That's not very sexy, is it?' I said.

I signed up Mike Tyson and Jean-Claude van Damme to do some ads and told Sean he had to get a sexier image. I think maybe he took me too literally. These days I'm advising him on how to deal with allegations that Ultra Tune's advertising is too sexy.

You never knew who you were going to meet at a Mike Tyson function. A despicable chap named Khaled Sharrouf came along to one of the dinners. He became an ISIS terrorist who earned worldwide condemnation when pictures of his seven-year-old son holding the severed head of a Syrian soldier were uploaded to the internet.

In Sydney I took Mike to Our Big Kitchen, a community

kitchen run by a Jewish organisation at Bondi. It feeds the homeless and offers support for troubled youth. I had arranged for Mike to speak to the disaffected young people. He was amazing. He stood in front of them and said, 'I was where you are'.

They sat spellbound as Mike told them about his life and the mistakes he had made. He didn't hold back. His language was the language of the street. There were plenty of profanities and I think some of the older people there were shocked, but not the kids. He delivered a very powerful message, and they hung on every word.

Every day I was with Mike he surprised me in one way or another. In Adelaide when we arrived at the airport there was a reporter from the *Advertiser* newspaper waiting to try to speak to him. You can imagine how intimidating it must be asking Mike Tyson for an unscheduled interview. The young man asked Mike if he could have a word.

'Sure,' Mike said and they started talking as we walked through the terminal. When we got into the lift to go down to the next level the reporter stopped. Mike put his hand against the doors to hold them open and said, 'You coming?' and the reporter stepped in too.

They talked in the lift and as we walked to the car, then Mike shook his hand and said 'see you later'.

Baddest man on the planet? Not that day.

In fact, not the whole time he was with me. Nothing was too much trouble. Interviews? No problem. Sign some items to auction for charity? Absolutely. One time I had about 50 pairs of boxing gloves and 100 photos piled up in the hotel room and he sat there signing them like a machine.

As I said earlier, apart from scheduled appearances, Mike only left his PlayStation on two occasions. In Melbourne I took the family out on a boat cruise, and in Perth we went out to lunch.

It was in Melbourne that I had the chance to sit down and have a chat with Kiki.

Mike and Kiki had known each other for 17 years but had been married for three when I met them. She is a wonderful woman who Mike credits with turning his life around.

As we were talking I told her what a great guy I thought Mike was, so warm and funny and good to be around. What she told me came as a shock.

She said that most nights when Mike goes to bed Kiki has to put her arms around him and comfort him because he is so sad and scared and unconfident. The man who was once the most feared fighter in the world needs reassurance that he can go to sleep knowing everything will be okay.

That certainly wasn't a side of Mike I ever saw. By the time we flew back to Sydney from Perth for their flight home to Vegas we were getting along famously. Not just me and Mike, but the whole family. The kids were beautiful and I would always try to entertain them when we were together. That day as we waited in the lounge at Sydney airport I asked them if they could walk like penguins.

'No,' they said, so I showed them.

I started waddling along with my feet splayed outwards, my arms straight down the sides of my body and my hands going flap-flap.

As I went across the room they fell into single file. Milan was doing the penguin behind me and Morocco was waddling along behind her. Then I looked back and saw, bringing up the rear, penguin-walking with a big smile on his face, the former undisputed heavyweight champion of the world, the baddest man on the planet: Mike Tyson.

What a lovely guy. Sweet, funny and what a worker. I've never seen anyone pose for as many pics on a photo line as he did — although Arnold Schwarzenegger tells me he once did 3,500 in four hours.

And that, my friends, is what we in the business call a segue.

ON THE ROAD WITH BILL CLINTON

Eating sweets and singing songs with President Bill Clinton on Sydney Harbour, as you do, 8 September 2001.

Oscar winner Al Gore meets Oscar nominee Toni Collette in Sydney, 19 September 2007.

ON THE ROAD WITH BILL CLINTON

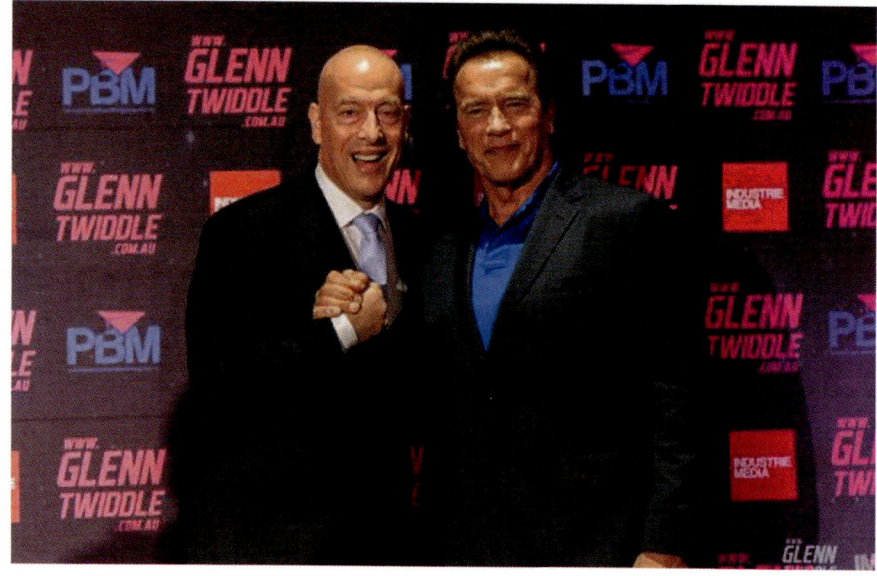

Max — I'll be back! Arnold Schwarzenegger in Sydney, 21 March 2017.

Britney Spears' bodyguard 'Fat Tony' Berretto and LA Lawyer Gloria Allred in New York, 24 September 2007.

ON THE ROAD WITH BILL CLINTON

With Rudy Giuliani flitting around Australia on the News Corp jet, 28 August 2003.

Chicago, Chicago! With Kim Kardashian in Chicago, 19 October 2010.

An evening with the lady in red, Raquel Welch, for the Children's Hospital at Westmead (Town-crier Graham Keating photobombing us) in Sydney, 1 March 2000.

Above: Backing a winner at the Melbourne Cup lunch with President George Bush Snr in Sydney, 6 November 2001.
Left: Thank you card from President George Bush Snr, 12 December 2001.

Left: The delightful Rachel Hunter in Sydney for the Children's Hospital at Westmead, 22 March 2007.

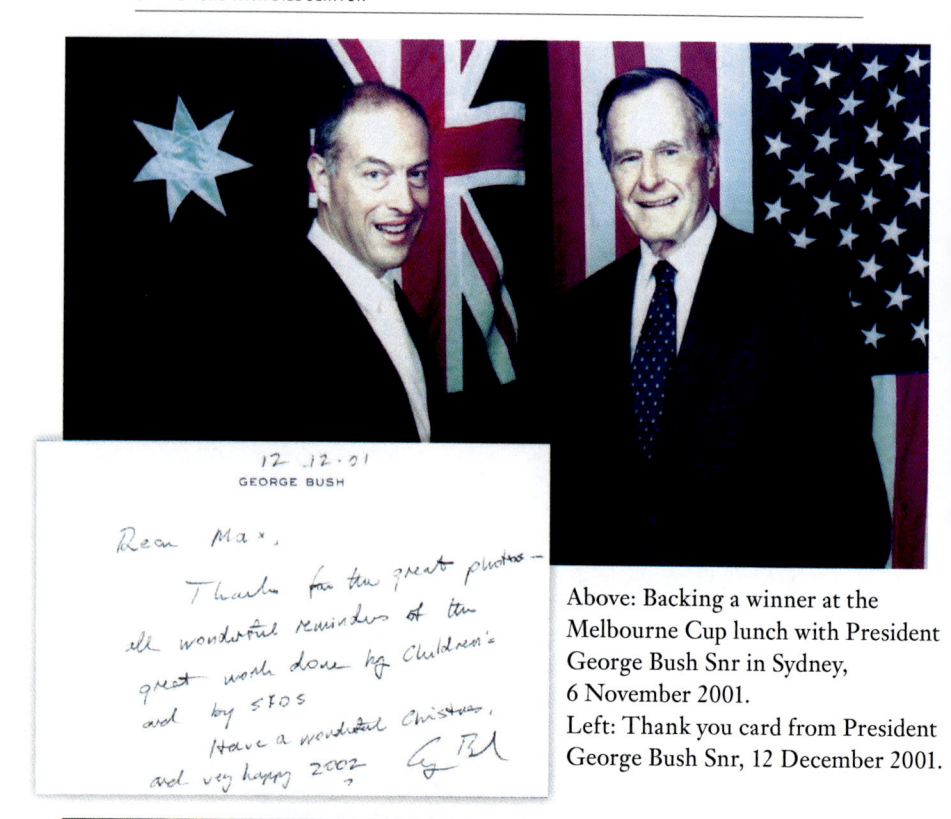

Right: Getting ready for Pamela Anderson's Big Brother news conference at the Pallazzo Versace on the Gold Coast, 9 July 2008. Photo by Paul Broben.

ON THE ROAD WITH BILL CLINTON

Tour guide Max Markson with (L-R) Lionsgate founder Frank Giustra, businessman and philanthropist Vinod Gupta, President Bill Clinton and Doug Band at the Sydney Opera House forecourt, 21 February 2006.

Above: Flying high to New York after the Muhammad Ali Centre Gala opening in Louisville, Kentucky, 19 November 2005.

Right: Playing MC and introducing Tony Blair at Anthony Pratt's apartment in Sydney, 30 July 2011.

ON THE ROAD WITH BILL CLINTON

A letter from Oprah Winfrey. Now that's class. 25 April 2013.

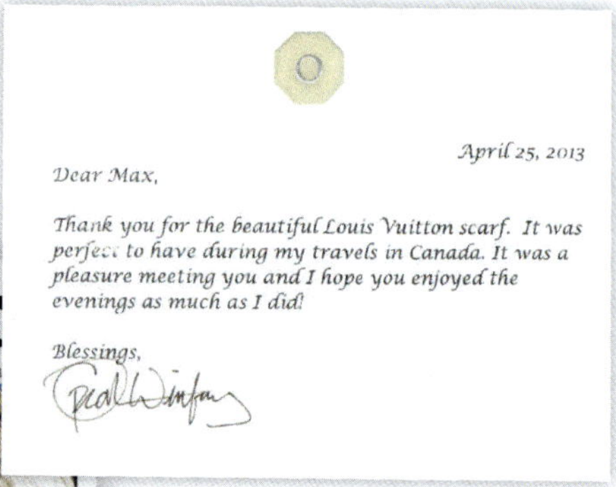

April 25, 2013

Dear Max,

Thank you for the beautiful Louis Vuitton scarf. It was perfect to have during my travels in Canada. It was a pleasure meeting you and I hope you enjoyed the evenings as much as I did!

Blessings,

Oprah Winfrey

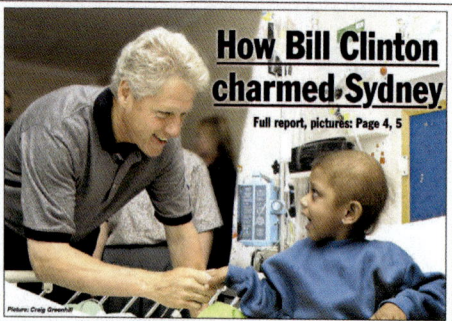

Both the *Sunday Telegraph* and the *Sun Herald* newspapers splashed their front pages with Bill Clinton on 9 September 2001.

ON THE ROAD WITH BILL CLINTON

Three events in two days with Nelson Mandela. Sydney, 4 September 2000.

Nelson Mandela, Kerry and James Packer and friends. An amazing lunch in Sydney, 4 September 2000.
Back row (L-R) Robbie Schiener, Daniel Petre, Ruffy Geminder, Adam Taylor, Peter Yates, Lynnda Sarinske, Graham Burke, Kerry Packer, Ashok Jacob, Wayne Passlow, David Gyngell, John Singleton, Mike Tilley, Steve Killelea, Chris Mackay, Robert Whyte, Brad Keeling, David Gonski, Jodee Rich, Bill Ireland.
Front row (L-R) Nelson Mandela, Richard Lubner, James Packer.

Scoring with Pele in Sydney, 27 March 2015.

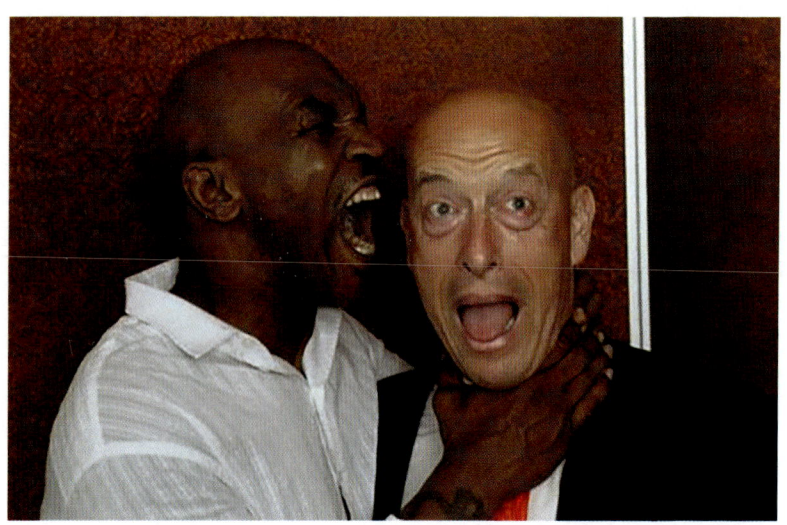

Mike Tyson putting the bite on me in Adelaide, 20 November 2012.

CHAPTER 9
HASTA LA VISTA, ARNIE
ARNOLD SCHWARZENEGGER (2013-2018)

When my plans to bring Arnold Schwarzenegger to Australia in 2010 came to nothing I told his agent, 'I'll be back', and three years later, I was.

A friend of mine, Jamie Mcintyre, wanted Arnold to come and speak at a series of financial education conferences he held annually, and I did the deal for June 2013. One of the conditions in the contract was for Arnold to do one hour of advance media interviews at a mutually agreed time and place to promote his visit.

In April 2013 Jamie and I went over to LA and had Arnie in a TV studio for a series of crosses to Australia.

It was the first time he'd met me and I don't think he was that impressed when his agent introduced me with the words, 'Arnold, this is Max Markson. He's very famous — he's been on *Celebrity Apprentice* in Australia.'

Little did we both know that one day Arnold would be stepping into President Donald Trump's shoes and hosting the US version of the show, but I guess that's for another book.

It was mid-afternoon in California at the time but early morning in Australia, and the schedule went like this:

From 7am to 7.10 we did a pre-record interview with

Larry Emdur and Kylie Gillies to be shown later on Channel 7's *The Morning Show*.

From 7.10-7.20 was live to air with David Koch and Melissa Doyle on *Sunrise*.

From 7.20-7.40 we did another pre-record to go nationally on *Today Tonight* that night. By then we were running a couple of minutes late and I could hear the producer of the *Today* show Neil Breen going crazy, screaming, 'Where's my Arnold Schwarzenegger interview?'

We get to it, and first Richard Wilkins does the interview but then Karl Stefanovic and Lisa Wilkinson take over because Karl wants to do his Arnie impersonation, which he does. Arnold smiles politely as he must do about 100 times a day when someone says, 'get to the chopper'.

After that we do some radio crosses and a phone interview with a reporter from News Corp in Sydney who had sent a photographer to the studio from their LA bureau to take a picture to go with it.

By then I've stretched the hour by about ten minutes but as we are leaving Channel 10 has got a film crew in the car park and Arnold is good enough to answer a couple of questions for them as well.

We got massive publicity and Arnold arrived at Sydney airport with his right-hand man Daniel Ketchell on Wednesday 12 June 2013.

The schedule of the conferences was for Arnold to speak in Perth on Wednesday night, Sydney on Thursday and Melbourne on Friday. He was in good company. Previous speakers I'd arranged had included Virgin boss Richard

Branson and entrepreneur Tim Ferris who has made a fortune out of his series of '4-Hour' books.

It was the second time I had met Arnold but the first time I had a chance to really get to know him. He is an absolutely fascinating character. Everything he does, he does with planning, application and precision.

A perfect example is the way he travels. When I met him at the airport we had to go from the international terminal to the domestic for the flight to Perth. As he walked out of customs he was carrying an overnight bag.

'Where is your luggage?' I asked.

'This is it,' he said and kept walking.

A seasoned traveller, he always packs light so that he doesn't have to waste time waiting to collect his luggage.

He has a great sense of humour and loves practical jokes. I didn't know this at first, but I soon found out.

As we were sitting in the Qantas Chairman's lounge waiting to board the flight to Perth he was on his iPad talking via Skype to a friend back in the States.

'I've flown all the way to Sydney,' he was saying, 'and now someone...'

He raised his voice and gave me a look straight out of *The Terminator*.

'*Someone...* says I have to fly right across the entire country to Perth.'

For a moment there I thought I was in trouble but then he gave me a lovely smile and a wink.

Normally Arnold speaks about the environment and politics but for this tour he had prepared a special talk about success. It's something he knows a lot about. There aren't too many people in the world who have been so successful in so many fields as Arnold: sport, business, entertainment, politics, he has reached the very top in everything he has done.

On the flight across to Perth he gave me a little insight into how he has achieved what he has. As I said before, nothing happens by chance.

We were sitting in our business class seats and I was running through the itinerary. The plan was that before each event we would have a photo line. I was explaining to him how it would work and he said, 'That's ok. I know photo lines. I do 400 pictures in 45 minutes.'

Now I'd been organising photo lines for 12 years at this point and I couldn't imagine that getting through that many photos in that little time was remotely possible. I didn't say that out loud of course. Telling Arnold Schwarzenegger that he is full of you know what whilst strapped into a seat next to him didn't seem like it would be good for my health.

'That's amazing,' I said. 'How is that possible?'

'Easy,' he told me. 'You know, when people wait to have their photo taken with you they always stand three steps away. When the previous photo is finished, that person leaves and the next one takes one, two, three steps over to you. I worked out that they can stand one step away and still not be in the picture, so I make sure that whoever is in charge of the photo line has the people stand exactly one step away. It saves a lot of time. My record is 3,500 people in one photo line.'

He told me that was at the first Arnold Classic — the bodybuilding symposium which has since grown into the Arnold Sports Festival and is held in Melbourne each year. It was thirty years ago in Columbus, Ohio and as part of the show they decided to sell 200 VIP tickets that included a photo with Arnold.

'The 200 tickets sold out in a few minutes,' he told me. 'So, we added another 200, and they sold out. So, another 200, and another and another. Finally, 3,500 in one afternoon. World record.'

It's like that with everything he does. One morning in Sydney we were having breakfast and he told me about the first time he was in the city.

At the time he was just making a name for himself outside the closed little world of body-building. Back in those days body-building was seen as a very strange and suspect past-time. It wasn't until Arnie and a couple of other champion body-builders like 'The Hulk' Lou Ferrigno, starred in the movie *Pumping Iron* that the sport became mainstream.

Before then, Arnie and others like him were beating their heads against a brick wall trying to gain attention and publicity. In Sydney, the local body-builder flying the flag for the sport was Paul Graham who would do anything to get his name and body into the paper or on TV — including wrestling a crocodile. To gain attention for one of his contests Paul brought Arnold, the reigning Mr Universe, to Sydney. At the end of the visit Paul paid Arnold about $1,500 in cash. Now many young men footloose and fancy free in a foreign country having just been handed a pile of cash might have blown it all on a good time. Not Arnold. He did what he did whenever a promoter anywhere in the world gave him money.

'I put it in my boots,' he said. 'Wherever I went, I told them I wanted cash and I put it in my boots so that when I walked through the airport to go home I knew exactly where it was. Then, when I got home I invested it in real estate.'

To those who would see him flexing his biceps at the beach or working out with weights, Arnold might have seemed like just another over-muscled gym junkie. What they didn't realise was that he was an astute property investor and developer cannily building up a portfolio that had made him a multi-millionaire long before he ever went to Hollywood.

Which brings us to the next chapter in the Arnold success story — a story that he told three nights running in his speech at the financial education conference.

About that speech: the first night in Perth I was with him in his dressing room as he sat and went through the speech in preparation for his appearance. He read it to himself, underlined passages that he wanted to emphasise, made notes and adjustments and then read it through again and again until he was 100 per cent happy with it. Nothing so unusual about that, you say? Of course he would need to get it right on the first night, you say?

Maybe, but the thing that really impressed me was that he did the exact same thing every night. The speech was the same, but he never stopped working on it, trying to make it even better, always striving to improve.

The speech started with Arnold telling the crowd that from his experience audiences were the same the world over.

'Forty per cent want to hear me speak about the environment,' he said. 'Fifty per cent want to hear about politics... and ten per cent just want their money back for *Hercules in New York* — but you're not getting it.'

He then gave his five tips for success:

Have a vision.

'I wanted to be a body-builder, I wanted to be a movie star.'

Think big.

'I didn't want to be any old body-builder, I wanted to be Mr Universe. I didn't want to just be in the movies, I wanted to be a leading man in the movies. I didn't want to be the Mayor of Carmel, I wanted to be the President. Okay, I couldn't be the President because I wasn't born in the United States, so I wanted to be Governor of California.'

Don't listen to the Nay-sayers.

'When I got to Hollywood they said, 'forget it. You'll never be a leading man. Look at your body. You might play a bodyguard or a soldier, but you'll never be the star. And what about that accent? No leading man in movies has ever had an Austrian accent, and what's your name? Schwartzenschnitzel? You've got to be joking. You'll never see that on a billboard.'

Work your butt off.

'When I started in movies if the director wanted me to crawl through the dirt over broken glass I'd do it, over and over again until I got it right. They would say, 'Arnold are you sure you want to do this again?' and I'd tell them, 'I'll do it until it's perfect. I want to be as good as I can possibly be.'

Give back.

'When I was at the peak of my career as an actor, the biggest star in Hollywood, I turned my back on it all to serve the people. California had been good to me, and I wanted to repay it. They asked me what they should do with the Governor's salary. I said, "keep it. Put it into public works".'

That, in a nutshell, was Arnold's speech, and it was fantastic. There is nothing more powerful than having someone stand up in front of you as living proof that everything he says is not only true, but achievable.

I refer a lot to that speech in business meetings, because everyone can relate to it. You have to think big, you have to work hard, and you have to ignore the knockers because in everything you do they are always going to be there. As for the final point — Give Back — I've spent a lot of my working life enabling people to do just that. I believe that nearly everyone feels they don't do enough to help others. I see my charity fundraising work as providing them with a means and opportunity to achieve that, and I never cease to be amazed, or moved, by how generously they respond.

Each night Arnold would follow his speech with a question and answer session — and every night, without fail the first question would be, 'Arnold, what is your favourite movie quote?'

Ever the showman he would give the room what it

wanted, and reel them off, 'Hasta la vista baby', 'Get to the chopper' and, of course, 'I'll be back'.

He then tells the story about how he and *The Terminator* writer-director James Cameron had disagreed over what would become one of the most famous lines in Hollywood history. You have to remember *The Terminator* was only the second movie that Cameron had ever made. In the days before *Titanic* and *Avatar* he was a virtual unknown. Arnold, on the other hand, had just made *Conan the Barbarian* and thought he knew quite a bit about the filmmaking business. So much so that he didn't think he should play the villain in *The Terminator*, he should play the hero, Reece. Thankfully Cameron talked him around, but then they had another difference of opinion over what became the movie's signature line.

'I thought it should be "I will be back",' Arnold said. 'Jim told me to stick to the script and say it the way he'd written it. I told him I didn't think it sounded right. I was supposed to be a machine. A machine wouldn't speak in abbreviations. He said, "Arnold, trust me." I had one more try and then he said, "Arnold, I don't tell you how to act. Don't tell me how to write." I admit it, I was wrong and now I can't go anywhere in the world without someone asking me to say, "I'll be back".'

After the speech we had a reception for about 20 people who had paid to spend some time with Arnold and then he and I and Ketch went to the bar at Perth's Crown Casino where we were staying. I bet you're wondering how hard those Hollywood superstars party, right? Well, I'm not sure what anyone else does, but Arnold had one glass of wine, a bit of small talk and headed off to bed.

The next morning, I went to the gym nice and early with my training partner Arnold Schwarzenegger then we flew by private jet to Sydney. We'd been together a couple of days by now and we'd got to that stage where we were pretty comfortable with each other and that flight back to Sydney gave us a good chance to have a chat. These are the times I really love. It's only away from all the cameras and the autograph hunters that these celebrities can really be themselves and Arnie is a great storyteller.

We were talking about the Kennedys and he told me that I had to get hold of the book *Sarge* written by his former father-in-law Sargent Shriver who had died in January 2011. Just months earlier Arnold and Maria, his wife of over 25 years had separated.

Even so, listening to Arnold speak about Maria and her family on the plane that day it was clear how much love and respect he has for them.

Not that they always had love for him. He told me that when he announced on *The Jay Leno Show* that he was running for Governor of California it came as something as a shock to the Kennedys, especially as they are Democrats and he is a Republican. Apparently one of them took it particularly hard: Bobby Kennedy Jnr. According to Arnold, young Kennedy had felt it was his birthright to be California governor and if anyone was going to be standing for election it should have been him.

I asked Arnold what he'd said about that. He just

shrugged and said, 'I told him. You schnooze, you lose.'

It was also on that flight that Arnie talked about the Arnold Classic and how it had grown from that first bodybuilding event in Columbus, Ohio to a massive sport expo held in Brazil, Spain and South Africa as part of his worldwide fitness crusade.

'You should get involved Max,' he said. 'Why don't you bring it to Australia?'

I told him it wasn't really my thing, but maybe I could put him together with someone better suited, and if it came off I could handle publicity and look after Arnold. Which is exactly how it turned out, but first we still had two shows to do.

First up was Sydney. We checked into the Darling Hotel and Ketch and I went out to the Hordern Pavilion where the event was being held to do a walk-though. On this occasion we had to take special care because there was another big-name celebrity involved. A few months earlier I had asked the US Ambassador Jeffrey Bleich if he would like to introduce Arnold to the crowd.

'Sure,' he said, and flew up from Canberra for the night.

All went very well. We had the photo line, Ambassador Bleich did his bit and Arnold's speech was even better than it had been the night before. Which was hardly surprising, because he'd spent time in his dressing room going over it again.

I asked him if he ever thought enough preparation was enough.

'Never,' he said. 'It's like riding a motorbike.'

I told him, 'You mean riding a bike.'

'No,' he said. 'Motorbike. In *Terminator II* I had to ride a motorbike and use a machine gun at the same time. I started practising six weeks before we shot the scenes and practised hour after hour after hour until I got it perfect. I do that with everything I do.'

Earlier in the day I had booked a table at a Japanese restaurant at the Darling for dinner after the show. When we got there it was empty. The lights were off and the chef had gone home. The owner was out the back. He came in to tell us he was closed, saw Arnie and just like magic, the lights came back on, the chef re-appeared and we had the most beautiful meal. Sometimes it helps to hang with the Terminator.

The next morning Arnie told me that when he had been in Sydney all those years ago he and Paul Graham had some publicity photos taken at Kirribilli, with the Opera House in the background.

'Let's go back there and take some new shots,' he said.

As we were leaving the casino I saw a freelance paparazzi named Andrew Murray waiting around hoping to get a shot of Arnold. It was about to be his lucky day. I pointed him out to Arnold and asked if we should take him along with us.

'Sure,' he said, gesturing to Andrew. 'You. Get in the chopper... I mean the car.'

We found the spot and Andrew took some nice shots. Arnie picked out the ones he wanted and Andrew sold the others. What you call a win-win.

Next stop was Melbourne. Same-same. Walk-through,

speech rehearsal, photo-line, speech, Q&A, 'Get to the chopper', 'Hasta la vista, baby', 'I'll be back'... I tell you, the man has the patience of Job.

There was one important difference to this night's agenda though. A friend of mine named Tony Doherty was there and he was super keen to meet Arnie. Tony owns the six Doherty's gyms around Melbourne and is obviously a huge Schwarzenegger fan. I told him I'd try to arrange to get him a couple of minutes. It then dawned on me that while I wasn't the right man to bring Arnold's Fitness Expo to Australia, Tony was. Long story short, Tony met Arnold, Arnold met Tony and that's how the Arnold Multi Sports Festival came to Melbourne in 2015, and every year since.

It just gets bigger every year, and that's saying something. That first year in 2015 we took Arnold out to the Australian Grand Prix — and he ended up presenting the trophy to the winner Lewis Hamilton.

Walking through the Expo with him is like nothing I've ever experienced before or since — and that includes walking along with President Clinton. There are crowds of tens of thousands of people there, and when Arnold walks around it's like a stampede. Everyone wants to see him and, if possible, touch him, shake his hand, ask him to sign something or say 'I'll be back'. That's why when he walks he is surrounded — and I mean surrounded — by security guards.

We call it 'the bubble'. No one gets in unless Arnold says, and once you're in, you can't get out until he gives the ok. It's quite amazing. A reporter might want to ask a question or take a photo. They see me in the bubble and call out,

'Max?' I ask Arnie if he'll talk to them and if he says ok the bubble opens just long enough for them to jump in. Then we all keep moving along until Arnold wants to stop, say to visit one of the sponsors' stands for a photo. The bubble opens, Arnold gets out, does what he wants to do, gets back in, the bubble closes again and off we go.

Incidentally, Arnold is not big on autographs. He'll do them if he has to but it's not part of what he does, like say Mike Tyson or Pele.

On that first trip to Melbourne we had arranged for him to do some signings and a photo line at a gym in a place called Derrimut which was miles from nowhere. I wasn't sure what to expect, and the further from the city we drove the more uncertain I was becoming. Then, when we got there I couldn't believe my eyes. It was the biggest gym I've ever seen in my life. It was the size of an aircraft hangar. They had a gigantic photo of Arnold on one wall. It must have been three storeys high. To sign it they had to raise him up on a scissor lift. There must have been 1,000 people there. It was incredible.

Those three days with Arnold I had been asking him to sign some photos that I wanted to auction at my charity events. No matter when I asked, it just didn't seem to be the right time. 'Not now Max,' he'd say. 'Later.' Day after day. 'Not now, later.'

Finally, it got to the stage where I was carrying all these photos with me when I took him to the airport for his flight back to the States.

'Now?' I asked him.

'Not now Max, later.'

We got to the airport, he checked in, picked up his little overnight bag and was just about to walk through into the customs area when he turned and took the photos and pen from my hand.

'Now Max,' he said, and gave me that smile and wink I had seen on day one.

He's a lovely guy. In July 2015 when he came out to Australia to promote *Terminator Genisys*, the last film in the series, his people sent me an invitation to attend the showing in Sydney. I went along, found my seat and cheered and clapped like everyone else when Arnie came out on stage. Given the cinema was absolutely packed I thought it was strange that there was a spare seat next to me but didn't pay much attention to it. Then Arnie went off stage, the lights went down and the movie started.

Next thing I knew the seat next to me was filled. By Arnold.

It was nice to be back in the bubble with the Terminator.

CHAPTER 10
GOOOOAAAALLLL
PELE (2015)

If you've made it this far you will know that I'm a big believer in the power of celebrity. Whether it's launching a new flavour of ice cream or selling tickets for a charity luncheon, nothing works better than having a celebrity name and face on your media release. The bigger the name, the better known the face, the more success you'll have.

In 2014 when a friend of the soccer commentator Les Murray approached me with the idea of holding a function to mark Les's retirement from SBS after a long and glorious career, I said sure — and started thinking about who we could get to be our celebrity star.

I usually start at the top and work down in these situations but in this case I started at the top and stayed there: Pele. The greatest footballer of all time was the first name that came to mind and, as luck would have it, we scored.

When I approached Les and suggested Pele, he was very excited. Not only had he interviewed Pele in the past and therefore already had a relationship with him, he had just been covering the FIFA World Cup in Rio and somehow got hold of Pele's agent's business card.

I gave the agent a call and asked if Pele would be interested in coming to Australia to do one function.

'Sure,' she said. 'How much are you offering?'

I told her US$50,000. When she stopped laughing I asked her how much it would take. She came back with some astronomical figure and when I picked myself up off the floor I said there was no way I could pay that much for just the one function.

'Why not do more than one then?' she asked, and we were off to the races.

Eventually we made a deal for four functions over two days at a fee of US$350,000. We would do a corporate lunch and public theatre show in Melbourne on the first day, and exactly the same in Sydney the next, all in honour of Les. The idea was that Les, who sadly died in 2017, would interview Pele at the lunches and former Socceroo and Premier League goal-keeper Mark Bosnich would introduce him at the evening shows.

We signed contracts, came up with a theme for the show: *Pele — My Life Story* and I booked the Peninsula in Melbourne and the State Theatre in Sydney.

Let me run that last one by you again: the State Theatre, one of the oldest, most famous and spectacular venues in the country. Opened in 1929 and touted as 'The Empire's Greatest Theatre' it has hosted everyone from Rudolph Nureyev to Bette Midler to the Sydney run of *Evita*. Suddenly I was more than a celebrity speaking agent and PR and promotions man. I was a theatre impresario. This was exciting. Music, lights, action. I could see it all… actually, I couldn't see it. I've done hundreds of lunches in my time. I can do them with my eyes closed. I'm the Andrew Lloyd Webber of lunches, but when it came to putting on a theatre show I was a complete novice and that wasn't going to cut it. When people pay to come to a charity lunch they expect either the chicken or the fish. When they pay for a theatre show they expect either *Phantom of the Opera* or *Cats*.

This was out of my league so I called in an expert, former TV executive producer Peter Adams, and he was fantastic. Peter put together a show that Pele should have taken around the world it was that good.

Peter researched all the major events in Pele's life and put them together into an interactive show in which the great man himself could talk and explain and demonstrate how he had come from poverty to become one of the most famous and popular sportspeople in the world.

For instance, when Pele was young he and his mates were so poor that not only didn't they have shoes, they didn't have a football. To play the game they loved they would steal clothes off a clothesline, roll them up and put them into a stocking to make a ball. Peter had written a script so that while Pele was telling this story he would actually be taking clothes off a clothesline, rolling them up and making a ball, just like he had as a kid.

There was a scene in which Pele re-enacted the chapter of his life when he was 9 years old and he and his father were listening to the final of the 1950 World Cup in Brazil. Brazil had the most fantastic team and they were expected to win after beating Sweden 7-1 and Spain 6-1 but the players were not permitted to play their natural game in the final against Uruguay. The Brazilian authorities told them they must play European style, and they were beaten 2-1.

Pele told of how his father was crying at the end of the game and he said, 'Dad, don't worry. One day I will win you a World Cup.'

He did better than that, he won three.

The story goes on, to the 1958 World Cup in Sweden where Pele became an overnight superstar, and through all the highlights of his amazing life and career, supported with film and still photos of Pele with world leaders and celebrities like the Kennedys, the Royal Family and Muhammad Ali.

The finale was Pele being joined on stage by a group of children and then giant inflatable footballs being kicked out into the crowd.

It was a wonderful show and we started advertising the two performances on 19-20 November. Tickets were going like hotcakes and we were selling signed shirts and boots on the website. All was going well. Then, a week before he was due to arrive, worldwide news: Pele rushed to hospital. A day later it's worldwide news again: Pele out of hospital.

By now it's Friday and he's supposed to be flying in on the Monday. I'm in a meeting and one of the people there says, 'Did you hear Pele is in hospital?' I said, 'No, it's fine. He's out.'

'No,' comes the reply. 'He's back in again.'

After the meeting I call Pele's agent and I'm told he's got serious kidney stone problems and we'll have to postpone the tour.

I say, 'Okay, can I have my money back?'

I've been an agent myself, and I know that giving money back is not something that agents like to do.

'No, no,' she says. 'We'll find some new dates.'

I have to contact everyone who has bought tickets and tell them that Pele won't be joining us as arranged, but that we will have new dates shortly. Two weeks later I am able to announce that he'll be coming in March, and it's all systems go.

Now comes the interesting part. I am suddenly drawn into the world of Pele, and it is a world unlike anything I have experienced before.

Pele's manager is a guy named Paul Kemsley, known universally as PK. He's an Englishman who was once a billionaire property developer who had also climbed to the very top of the football mountain. He was deputy chairman of Tottenham Hotspurs in the UK, and then bought the New York Cosmos, which is how he came into contact with Pele. PK's property company collapsed during the Global Financial Crisis but he made a profit on his sale of Cosmos, which he then invested into forming a sports management company which, at that time, had only one client. You guessed it: Pele. He even named it after Pele's shirt number, Legends 10.

Under the terms of Pele's agreement with PK's company, he sold them the rights to his name, face and image for an enormous amount of money and he has to make himself available for personal appearances, speaking engagements and to sign items, such as shirts, boots, balls and photos, for a certain number of days each year. It's not just a case of Pele saying, 'I've got a bit of time free next Tuesday, how about I sign a couple of things then?' It is a very strict routine, with Pele having the signing sessions locked into his schedule a year in advance. That means, wherever he is in the world at the set time, he has to stop what he is doing and start signing, and PK's people have to have the items ready to be signed whether he is in Brazil, Berlin or Bondi.

Sound silly? Well, consider this: Pele commands $300 a signature and he can sign up to 3,000 items per signing session. That's $900,000 a session. Serious money.

When I did the deal with PK, I put in a condition that Pele had to do some media interviews to promote the tour. That was fine, but it had to be done during the time already set aside for one of Pele's weekly signing sessions, otherwise they would have had to pay him extra. That was all very well in theory, but Pele wasn't in Australia, he was somewhere on the other side of the world and his signing session time that week happened to fall at around 3am Australian time. It says a lot about the power of Pele's name that Channel Nine's sports guru Ken Sutcliffe and Chris Smith from 2GB, amongst others, were prepared to set their alarms to be ready to record their interviews before the sun came up. *The Sydney Morning Herald* flew reporter Nick O'Malley from Washington to Brazil for an interview and I spent $8,000 on a TV truck and to buy satellite time so we could do live TV and radio crosses. All the while, the meter was running, with someone from Legends 10 standing beside Pele with a stopwatch making sure he didn't go outside his allotted signing session time because then it would start costing them money.

Things didn't always go smoothly. Some of the radio

interviews were a bit scratchy. Pele speaks perfect English but a journalist in Sydney and a football superstar in Santos talking over the top of each other on a dodgy phone line doesn't always make for great radio. Then there was the time that Pele decided to stretch his legs in the middle of an interview and didn't come back. So it was hard, but in the end it all worked.

Finally, Pele arrives, and not a moment too soon. Between when he was first scheduled to appear in November 2014 and when he eventually landed in Melbourne in March 2015, quite a bit had happened. For starters the venues I had booked weren't necessarily still available so I had to re-book — and lose my deposits. The US dollar had got stronger against the Australian dollar which was costing me money. I had to refund tens of thousands of dollars to people who had paid for the original shows but couldn't make the new dates, and I had to pay for a whole new advertising campaign.

Still, at least PK was willing to lessen the pain.

'Sorry about that,' he said. 'How about I give you 50 free shirts?'

Who said the world of big business doesn't have a heart?

We checked Pele into a suite at the Grand Hyatt. He was accompanied by Kane Swerner, one of PK's people from LA, plus Ben Brodie, a Cockney guy who was Pele's 'minder' — just like the character Dennis Waterman played in the TV show. When Ben and I got talking he told me his father once managed a band named Osibisa. I told him that when I was just starting out in the UK I promoted them.

Small world. I was footing the bill for Ben by the way, but I didn't mind. As Ben described it to me, security is like insurance. You never need it until you need it.

Just by chance the day that Pele arrived was one of his signing days. I headed up to the hotel suite with 10 replica World Cups that I'd got from Hong Kong, a few pairs of boots and my 50 free shirts. I was hoping it wouldn't be too much of a burden for him to sign, but when I walked in I couldn't believe my eyes. There were boxes of gear lining the walls, thousands of items that Kane had brought with him for Pele to sign as part of his contractual obligation. It was like watching a production line in a factory. The minder would keep the items moving along, Pele, sitting there in his hotel bathrobe, would sign them and Kane, for proof of authenticity, would take a picture. In my head I could hear the sound of a cash register each time he signed: ker-ching, ker-ching, ker-ching.

The next day we have the first of the functions, a $300-a-head ($700 with photo) round table luncheon for 400 guests with proceeds to Les's testimonial. Pele is fantastic. He was 74 at the time and he's just had his kidney stone issues but his smile lights up a room like nothing you've ever seen. He chats, he shakes hands, and is charming and funny in his interview with Les. Because he has hip problems he sits on a stool for the photo line, but he does everything asked of him. He and Ben are a good team. Ben knows exactly what Pele can do and what he can't do, and he is very protective of him. If someone is getting a little pushy or asking too much, he very quietly and unobtrusively steps in and steers them away.

After the lunch we took Pele back to the hotel to prepare for that night's theatre show, but before he went on stage we had another special engagement. The Make a Wish Foundation makes impossible dreams come true for sick kids and for one little boy in Melbourne that dream was meeting arguably the greatest footballer of all time. Pele was only too happy to do it and we arranged a private meeting between Pele, the boy and his parents before the show. He couldn't have been more generous with his time. They talked and laughed and he posed for a picture with them. It was really nice to see. He's a beautiful man.

The show was everything I had hoped for. It was absolutely brilliant, and the crowd loved it. That night we flew by private plane to Sydney to do the whole thing again the next day.

The Sydney luncheon was at Doltone House at Pyrmont. As with the corresponding function in Melbourne there was a private affair for 20 people with a bit of a meet and greet, a photo line and lunch for 700 guests, followed by Pele being interviewed on stage by Les. The MC for the theatre shows was former Aston Villa, Manchester United and Chelsea goalkeeper Mark Bosnich, and for the lunch events we had ex-Socceroo midfielder turned commentator Craig Foster.

When everyone had finished eating Craig got up and introduced Les who went up and sat in a chair waiting as Craig introduced Pele.

Pele, with Ben walking behind him, went to walk up the three steps onto the stage, but because of his hip problems he was a little wobbly on his feet. Craig stood there with his hand out to shake Pele's hand but just as he reached him, Pele stumbled. For some reason, Craig stepped back and Pele fell flat on his face as if he'd been shot.

A huge gasp went up around the room as Ben rushed up and helped Pele to his feet. Me? I could only think of one thing: 'Why did I book a midfielder? I should have got a keeper. Mark Bosnich would have caught him.'

He's a trouper though. After Ben helped him up Pele went over to his seat for the interview and carried on as if nothing had happened. I guess after the way the Bulgarians fouled and chopped him out of the 1966 World Cup he was used to hitting the deck.

With that unfortunate experience behind us Kane and I paid special attention when we did our walk-through of the State Theatre before that night's show. A walk-through is something I do with the talent's representative before any function. You can imagine how much importance Bill Clinton's people put on scoping out a venue where he is going to appear. Given what had happened at lunch Kane was even more attentive than usual and he took one look at the steps leading up to the stage and said there was no way Pele could use them. We tried out every possible alternative and decided the best thing to do was to use a funny little back entrance and a couple of steps that led down from the dressing rooms. That way we could have Pele waiting on stage behind the curtains before people even arrived.

It made things a little more involved but it all worked out and the show was another huge success. We got Pele back up the couple of steps and into the dressing room — and guess what he did then. Well, it just so happened that a couple of minutes after the show ended the clock ticked onto another signing session, and Kane was waiting with another pile of items to be signed.

I might add that signing footballs and shirts isn't the only way Pele makes money. He has a long list of blue chip sponsors that any athlete would kill for, including Coca-Cola, Emirates and Hublot watches. The year he was in Australia he just happened to be the number one player on EA Sports' mega-selling FIFA computer game, so they sponsored the theatre shows. I didn't have to pay for his travel to and from Australia either. He had been doing a function in Liverpool for Emirates before he came here, so they flew him to Australia, and he went straight to China for Hublot after he left so they footed the bill for getting there.

To say he had a full calendar is an understatement, but he didn't seem to mind. He appeared to genuinely love meeting people and they sure enjoyed meeting him.

To me he came across as a very down-to-earth honest and humble man who has never forgotten where he came from and is always happy to promote the game that gave him so much. When he shook my hand at Sydney airport before he flew out to China and gave me that famous smile I couldn't help but feel totally in awe.

There is a postscript to Pele's visit. Those ten replica World Cups that he signed were some of the most popular and profitable items I have ever sold at one of my charity events. It was a big fundraiser in Sydney and I offered one for $5,000. It sold in an instant, so I had the MC say to the crowd, 'don't worry, I've got another one'. That one sold too, and the next one, and the next one, until all ten had gone, bringing in $50,000 in about two minutes.

'How good is this?' I thought, and immediately ordered another ten from Hong Kong. When they arrived all safely packed in polystyrene containers I sent them straight over to Kane in the US who added them to the pile of items waiting to be put in front of Pele at his next signing session. At $300 a signature, plus the cost or purchase and shipping I figured I was still going to be a long way in front.

And I would have been too, if whoever sent them back to me had thought to put them back in those polystyrene containers. Instead they just shoved them in cardboard boxes and when I opened them up they were all cracked and broken. Probably about $5,000 down the drain.

I think Pele would say, that's what you call an own goal.

CHAPTER 11
RAQUEL, RACHEL AND PAMELA
(2000-2013)

As you can probably tell, of all the wonderful women I have worked with over the years Kim Kardashian holds a special place of honour. She is the total professional, always early, always prepared, and always looking a million dollars. Which is apt, because that's pretty much what she charges for a day's work.

Kim is just one of many incredibly talented ladies I have been lucky enough to spend time with in my career. A few stand out, like movie star, Raquel Welch.

Back in late 1999 I was getting a reputation for my charity functions and I got a call asking if I would do a fundraiser for the Children's Hospital at Westmead in Sydney. Of course, I was only too happy to put it together.

'Who do you want me to get as the star?' I asked.

'Someone famous from overseas,' came the reply.

That left me with plenty of scope.

As a kid I had always admired Raquel Welch. One of the bestselling posters in the world was of Raquel in that fur bikini from the movie *One Million Years B.C.* The poster of Raquel even appeared in the movie *Shawshank Redemption*. So, when I started thinking about 'someone famous from overseas', a vision of Raquel Welch appeared.

I did some phoning, tracked down her agent and arranged for her to come to Australia for three functions in March 2000.

As part of our deal Raquel had stipulated that she wouldn't do any media whatsoever. I didn't think that would be a major problem because she was such a big name and the Children's Hospital was such a good cause that the function would sell itself. I was right, tickets sold just on the strength of her name, but what I didn't count on was the fragile feelings of the local press. When I announced that Raquel was coming they naturally started contacting me and asking for interviews. When I said that wasn't possible there were numerous noses out of joint and by the time she arrived in the country the media coverage wasn't just tepid, it was bordering on toxic.

The first day that Raquel was in the country I had arranged to take her for a harbour cruise on stockbroker Rene Rivkin's magnificent boat. We had a wonderful afternoon with a select group, including Raquel's leading New York PR and publicity person Jacqui Becher. Jacqui and I were talking about how lovely Raquel was when I said to her: 'She is, but why are the media being so unkind to her?'

'It's obvious,' Jacqui said. 'It's because she hasn't done anything. Why don't you take her to the Children's Hospital?'

So that's what we did. The next day, before the function we went for a visit to the hospital and invited some reporters and photographers to come along.

All went well until Raquel was visiting with the children in the cancer ward and she became totally overwhelmed. I had to take her to a side room so she could have a cry without upsetting the kids.

Obviously it hadn't been a contrived thing, but her

very real and human reaction to the plight of these brave children and their families totally turned the media around. One minute they had been putting her down, the next they loved her.

That night we had the first function. MC for the night was Tony Barber, Australia's best-known game show host and one of the biggest names on the local entertainment scene.

So how did I introduce him?

'Raquel, this is Tony Barber. He's just had double hip surgery.'

He was not impressed.

Despite that classic case of Markson foot-in-mouth, the function was a roaring success.

Raquel came out on stage, charmed the audience, told some movie stories and did a Q&A. Then we had the auction which took us to a $150,000 profit on the night.

The major item was something that had taken me a lot of time and effort to put together: a framed collection of photographs and the original autographs of all 25 Australian prime ministers. As you can imagine, the living PMs weren't too much of a problem. The dead ones took some finding, but I managed. All except for one: prime minister number six, Joseph Cook. Try as I might, I just couldn't find a signature for the man who had run the country from June 1913 to September 1914. Finally, I had a breakthrough. Over the years I had become friends with former PM Sir Billy McMahon and his wife Lady Sonia. I mentioned my dilemma to Sonia and she told me that Joseph Cook's grand-daughter was still alive and living on the Gold Coast. I tracked her down and asked if by any chance she might have something with her grandfather's signature on it — a letter, Christmas card, gas bill. Anything.

She told me that she had only one thing: his original certificate of appointment as prime minister, framed and hanging on a wall at her home, and as it was for a good cause she would give it to me.

I almost hated to take it, but I simply had no choice. I arranged to have the certificate collected and when I got my hands on it I cut the signature out and had it placed in the frame underneath Joseph Cook's photograph. The night of the function Rene Rivkin bought the item at auction for $40,000.

About a week later I was surfing eBay looking for potential auction items for upcoming events and what do you think I found? Someone in the US was selling an authentic Joseph Cook signature for $20. I bought it, cut around the edges so that it was the right size, stuck it in the frame where the old signature had been and sent it back to the Gold Coast. If you don't get up too close, you can hardly tell the difference.

From Sydney we went to Melbourne, which was just as good as the first night, although it had the potential to be a disaster.

I had asked Eddie McGuire if he would be the MC and he readily agreed. He asked if we would put together some questions for him to ask Raquel in their interview, which we did. Then, at the last minute, he had to pull out.

'Don't worry,' he said. 'I've got Sam Newman to take my place.'

Which was, of course, when I started to worry.

Sam, as Forrest Gump might say, is like a box of chocolates — and not always in a good way. You never know what you're going to get, and over the years his interaction with women has got him into all sorts of strife.

Not this night. Sam arrived early, was fully prepared with Eddie's questions and a total gentleman.

Still, how could you not be when in the presence of Raquel Welch?

Finally, we flew to Brisbane. This time the MC was Kerri Anne Kennerley and everything went smoothly. Raquel was a delight, doing everything we asked — including something a little out of left field.

Entrepreneur Jim Raptis was building a huge residential and retail development on the Gold Coast at the time and part of it was a celebrity walk of fame with the handprints and signatures of famous people set in concrete, à la Grauman's Chinese Theatre in Hollywood. Jim had begged me to bring Raquel down to the Coast so she could put her hands in cement but I told him we couldn't fit it into her schedule.

'Fine,' said 'Jim. 'If Raquel won't come to the cement. I'll bring the cement to Raquel.'

Sure enough, just before Raquel walked into the room for her Brisbane appearance, all immaculately made up, wearing a stunning red dress and looking superb, she stopped just long enough to stick her hands into a waiting square of wet cement. Jim handed over a large cheque made out to the Starlight Founation, and it was on with the show.

Everything went smooth as silk. Well, apart from when I lost Raquel at Brisbane airport after arriving from Melbourne and I was running around like a lunatic screaming, 'has anyone seen Raquel Welch? Has anyone seen Raquel Welch?' that is. Don't worry, I found her.

I must say though, those days and nights I spent in her company made a great impression on me.

I no longer only have to hear her name to think of the movies *One Million BC* and *Shawshank Redemption*, instead I now see a 59-year-old woman in a red dress. And she's still every bit as incredible.

Speaking of incredible, the next woman on my list is certainly that, but Rachel Hunter gets a start not just for being a pretty face. She's here because of all the international celebrities I have ever worked with I rate her the most down to earth and delightful.

My connection with Rachel went back to 2002 when I started taking celebrity speakers to New Zealand and ended up renting space in the office of former All Black Andy Haden. Andy played over 100 games for the All Blacks and is a rugby legend in his homeland. None of which meant a thing to me. As far as I was concerned he was a talent agent who was very helpful when I started working in New Zealand. He was full of good advice, including that I should put on what turned out to be probably the most satisfying function I have ever done — a charity event in aid of the great New Zealand miler John Walker who won gold in the 1500m at the 1976

Montreal Olympics. In 1996 it was reported that John was suffering from Parkinson's Disease and Andy suggested I should organise an event in his honour.

It was an amazing evening. I had flown in the great British runners Sebastian Coe and Steve Ovett and also had a little surprise for John, and everyone else.

The MC had been interviewing John on stage about his career and had got to the story of the 1974 Commonwealth Games in Christchurch, where everyone in New Zealand was willing him to break the world record for the 1500m. He did break the record in that race, but so did the great Tanzanian runner Filbert Bayi, who got to the finish line just ahead of John in arguably the greatest 1500m race of all time.

Earlier Seb Coe had told the audience that Bayi and John had changed the face of 1500m racing for all time that day because instead of pacing himself and ending with a big burst at the end, Bayi had sprinted the whole way and John had gone with him.

'Obviously Filbert Bayi isn't here today but let's look at the video of that amazing race,' the MC said. The lights went down, the video played and everyone clapped.

Then the MC said, 'Actually John. I lied to you earlier. Filbert Bayi is here, and if you turn around, he's standing right behind you.'

The lights went up, the two men embraced, the crowd went wild. My finest moment.

Which is all a pretty long introduction to Rachel Hunter, who just happened to be one of Andy's clients. It seemed like an obvious thing to do so one day I said to Andy, 'why don't I do some charity events with Rachel?' So we did, one in Auckland and one in Sydney.

We called them 'An Evening with Rachel Hunter' and raised a nice pile of money for Starship, the children's hospital in Auckland and the Children's Hospital at Westmead in Sydney.

Other than one of my biggest ever foot-in-mouth faux pas (and by now you'd know that's a pretty big field) it would have been perfect. It was at the Sydney function and I spotted a famous fashion designer walking towards me.

'Hello,' I said kissing her cheek and looking at her tummy. 'Congratulations, I didn't know you were pregnant.'

She wasn't. What's that expression about wanting the ground to open up and swallow you? Still, even that moment of abject embarrassment couldn't dim my enjoyment of working with Rachel. She was just so nice, so sincere and natural with no airs and graces. Being with Rachel Hunter is like being with the girl next door. If the girl next door is an international supermodel *Sports Illustrated* swimsuit edition cover-girl once married to Rod Stewart that is.

Did someone say swimsuit? Pamela Anderson joined the Markson circus in July 2008.

Back then the hottest show on TV was *Big Brother*, filmed on the Gold Coast with Kyle Sandilands and Jackie O hosting. The show's producers had approached me about getting some celebrities to come into the *Big Brother* house and I had just the man. Or the boy, anyway. You know how

Andy Warhol said everyone would have 15 minutes of fame? Well, in March 2008 Corey Worthington was having his, big time. Corey had become famous for holding a party when his parents had left town for the night. Around 500 people showed up, it was bigger than Ben Hur and when a TV interview of a mono-syllabic and unrepentant 16-year-old Corey went viral on YouTube he became an internet sensation. Even before the house was cleaned up after the party, I was Corey's manager and I signed him up for 10 days in the *Big Brother* house for $50,000.

As luck would have it I had already lined up US fashion designer, *Queer Eye For The Straight Guy* TV star and gay icon Carson Kressley for some gigs with Myer and did a deal for him to spend one night in the house. The ratings tripled so I signed him for another night at a suitably inflated fee.

'Who else do you want?' I asked the producers.

'Who have you got?' they said.

I pitched *American Pie* star Tara Reed but they felt her 15 minutes was up and passed.

'What about Pamela Anderson?'

They loved it.

'Can you get her?' they asked.

'Of course I can,' I said, with absolutely no idea how to find her or whether she'd be interested.

I tracked down her manager Peter Asher and put it to him. For $250,000 for a couple of hours work a day she was very interested and she and Peter were on the next plane out of LA. I met them at Sydney airport and we waited in the

Chairman's Lounge for a flight to Brisbane.

Pamela was lovely and a lot of fun but I have to admit for that hour or so at Sydney airport I was more interested in Peter. The name Asher might not mean a lot to young people today but back in the 1960s it was bigger than huge. Jane Asher was a young singer whose boyfriend just happened to be Paul McCartney from a little band called The Beatles, and Peter Asher was her brother. In his teens Peter and a mate had started a singing duo called Peter and Gordon. They did pretty well. I guess it didn't hurt having Paul McCartney say 'here you go boys. I wrote this song with John Lennon, but you can have it'. When his performing days were over Peter worked for The Beatles' record company where he signed an unknown singer named James Taylor. He then moved to the States where he became number two at Sony. At some stage he moved to Malibu where his next-door neighbour was, you guessed it, Pamela Anderson. He ended up representing her and that's how the three of us ended up chewing the fat in Sydney.

'Tell me, what was it like having a sister going out with Paul McCartney?' I asked.

'Well,' he said. 'I always knew when he'd stayed over at our house. I'd look out the front curtains in the morning and the street would be full of screaming girls.'

Peter and Pamela were great company. When we arrived in Brisbane I had a limo waiting to take us down to the Palazzo Versace hotel on the Gold Coast. As always, I had bought her a present, which I gave her in the car.

Actually, to tell the truth I hadn't bought it for her. I had originally bought it for Burt Bacharach who I had met a month or so earlier that year. Burt is a big horse rider and I had purchased a whip at the Hermes store in Sydney. I later discovered that horse riders don't use whips, they use riding crops, so I bought him one of those instead, which left me with a $1,000 Hermes whip. I had been thinking long and hard about a gift for Pamela when it dawned on me that a whip would be perfect for her and she did love it too.

We got to the hotel and got ready for a media conference. When I went to pick her up from her room I was wearing a bright yellow tie. She came to the door in a baby doll yellow dress.

'Oh Max,' she said. 'We match.'

She did all the press, got mountains of publicity and then dropped into the *Big Brother* house a few times over two days. The ratings went through the roof. The producers couldn't have been happier. Well, maybe they could have been happier if Pamela hadn't decided to use some of her spare time to indulge in one of her major passions, animal rights.

Pamela is a big supporter of PETA — People for Ethical Treatment of Animals. Unbeknown to me, the local chapter had arranged to hold a protest outside a Gold Coast KFC outlet on one of the days Pamela was in town. She read about it in the paper and decided to go down and lend her support. Needless to say, it was the most publicised protest they'd ever had.

Did I mention that KFC was the major sponsor of *Big Brother*? Oh well, what can I say? That's showbiz.

Which brings us almost to the end of the road. We

started this book with the most admired man in the world, it's only fitting that we finish with the most admired woman, Oprah Winfrey.

In 2013, after I had overseen that hour of media interviews with Arnold Schwarzenegger in LA I flew straight to Ottawa to meet Oprah. I didn't get to speak to her that first night. I just watched her amazing show and was blown away like everyone else.

I was one of 12,000 people entranced by her. She is very personable, very inspirational.

She tells the parable of the feather, the brick and the bus — the moral being that we should listen to our body when it tickles us with a feather to let us know that we have to pay attention. If we don't, we're going to have a brick land on us, and if we still ignore the message there's going to be a bus coming around the next corner with our name on it.

She sits on a couch and speaks to the audience, every one of whom thinks she's talking directly to them. She gives away the pair of shoes that she has been wearing and does a Q&A with Canadian TV and radio personality George Stroumboulopoulos.

It might not sound like much, but you have to be there. It's cute, it's intimate. It's powerful and the audience loves it.

And boy is it profitable.

Before each show she does a meet and greet for 150 people at $850 a head. Add that to ticket sales for tens of thousands of people at sold-out shows night after night and you can see why Oprah is the richest women in America and why I was so keen to bring her to Australia.

The next morning, I flew to Montreal for her next show. As soon as I'd checked into my hotel I headed out shopping and bought her a beautiful Louis Vuitton scarf.

Before the show I went to meet her in her dressing room. Her agent had already told me that she wouldn't have a photo taken with me, which was understandable. I wouldn't want a photo with me either. She was very warm and friendly. I gave her the scarf and told how much I'd love to bring her to Australia.

'And I'd love to come,' she said.

Oprah had already been to Australia once before, in 2010 when she did her TV show from the front of the Sydney Opera House and Hugh Jackman hurt himself riding a flying fox down from one of the sails.

I told her I wanted her to do exactly the same show that she was doing in Canada, and offered US$5 million for five events.

She liked the sound of that and said she hoped we could work something out. So did I Oprah, so did I. We shook hands, she went on with getting ready. I found my seat and, once again, was one of 12,000 people sitting in the palm of her hand.

Sadly, the Max Markson-Oprah Winfrey tour of Australia never happened because she wanted a back-end deal. What that means is this: normally I pay an outright fee and whatever I sell the tickets for and whatever profit I make is my business.

Say for instance you're a big-time promoter and you've booked Ed Sheeran, what you do is guarantee him a certain amount against a percentage of the profits. Given that on his last tour of Australia Ed sold 1,000,000 tickets, that's going to be a lot of money.

Let's say you do a deal with Ed for a guaranteed $50 million against 90 per cent of the profits, which means after all the expenses have been paid 90 per cent of the profit goes to Ed and you get 10 per cent. If they gross $75 million and it costs say $5 million to stage the show there's $70 million profit. You get $7 million and Ed gets $63 million.

Oprah wanted to structure a deal like that, rather than what I wanted to do, which was fair enough. We went backwards and forwards, I went from four shows to six shows, up to $5.5 million, down to $4 million, but it just didn't happen.

And that, I thought, was the end of my dealings with Oprah Winfrey. Then one day a letter arrived at my office.

'Dear Max,' it read. 'Thank you for the beautiful Louis Vuitton scarf. It was perfect to have during my travels in Canada. It was a pleasure meeting you. I hope you enjoyed the evenings as much as I did. Blessings, Oprah Winfrey.'

Every time I read that letter I get to the word 'blessings' and smile.

It means a lot to me, because when I think of how far I've come and the amazing people that I've travelled along the road with, it says it all.

I'm blessed.

INDEX

A
Abbott, Tony 35
Abedin, Huma 56
Adams, Gerry 59
Adams, Peter 147
Abdulla, King 59
Albright, Madeleine 59
Ali, Muhammad 148
Allred, Gloria 69
Anderson, Pamela 164-167
Asher, Jane 166
Asher, Peter 165-166

B
Bacharach, Burt 167
Barber, Tony 159
Bayi, Filbert 163
Beatles, The 51, 97, 166
Becher, Jacqui 158
Bergman, Ingrid 51
Berretto, Anthony 70
Bin Laden, Osama 48
Blair, Cherie 104, 108, 1113-114
Blair, Leo 111
Blair, Tony 103-114, 116
Bleich, Jeffrey 139
Bogart, Humphrey 36, 51
Border, Allan 14
Bosnich, Mark 146, 153-154
Bush, Barbara 62-63
Bush, George W. 38, 45, 58, 62-64, 69
Bush Snr, George W. 8, 58, 61-64, 89
Bushnell, Candace 98
Brakensiek, Annalise 14

Band, Doug 38, 48, 50-51, 53-54, 56-57
Bradman, Ash 121
Branson, Richard 59, 131
Breen, Neil 130
Brodie, Ben 151-152
Brown Gordon 114
Buckley, Sean 125
Byrnes, Jim 42

C
Cairns, Gordon 81
Carman, Chris 116
Carr, Bob 22, 44
Carter, Jimmy 58
Carter, Reuben 15
Castro, Fidel 39, 107
Churchill, Winston 75-76
Clinton, Bill 8-9, 11, 27-59, 81, 84, 89, 92-93, 105, 108, 141, 154
Clinton, Chelsea 37, 40
Clinton, Hillary 40, 42, 56, 58-59, 75
Coates, John 20
Collette, Toni 68
Cook, Joseph 15-160
Corleone, Michael 93
Costello, Elvis 59
Cressley, Carlson 165
Crews, Rev Bill 24
Cuthbert, Betty 83

D
D'Amato, Gus 124
Danson, Ted 58
Diamond, Michael 41
Diana, Princess 61, 95, 110
Doherty, Tony 141
Doyle, Brian 48, 50, 54, 81-82, 108
Doyle, Melissa 130

E
Edge, The 58
Eisenhower, Ike 35
Eisman, Kathryn 98
Eisner, Michael 85-86
Elizabeth, Queen 51, 110
Emdur, Larry 130
Engelberg, Mort 32-38, 44-45, 47

F
Federline, Kevin 70
Fenech, Jeff 14, 17
Ferrigno, Lou 133
Ferris, Tim 131
Fiorina, Carly 85-86
Fishburn, Laurence 43
Foster, Craig 153
Fraser, Malcom 22
Freeman, Morgan 58
Friedberg, Ric 74-76, 78-79

G
Gaddafi 107
Gandel, John 79
Gandi, Mahatma 43
Gatto, Mick 125
Geminder, Raphael "Ruffy" 20

Gerry and the Peacemakers 97
Gillard, Julia 104
Gillies, Kylie 130
Giuliani, Judith 78, 82, 85
Giuliani, Rudy 8-9, 11, 73-86
Giustra, Frank 37
Givens, Robin 124
Glazer, Aram 37
Glen, John 59
Gomez, Selena 101
Gonski, David 19-20
Gore, Al 33, 664-71
Gore, Tipper 33
Goward, Pru 67
Graham, Paul 133, 140
Green, Sir Phillip 77
Gyngell, David 18

H
Hadley, Ray 43
Hamilton, Lewis 141
Hannah, Daryl 59
Haden, Andy 162-164
Hawke, Bob 18, 22, 68, 113-114
Hess, Mike 75
Hill, Michael 87-88, 90, 95, 97-98
Hope, Bob 23
Howard, John 67
Humphreys, Kris 95, 97
Hunter, Rachel 162-164
Hussein, Saddam 62

172

J
Jackman, Hugh 169
Jacob, Ashok 18
Jagger, Mick 58
Jenkins, Roy 75
Jenner, Caitlin 101
Jenner, Kendall 101
Jenner, Kris 101
Jenner, Kylie 100-101
John, Elton 51
Johnson, Ben 115
Johnson, John 32
Jones, Alan 48, 81-82

K
Kardashian, Khloe 101
Kardashian, Kim 101
Kardashian, Kourtney 101
Keating, Paul 43
Keeling, Brad 20
Kemsley, Paul 149
Kennedy, Bobby Jnr. 138
Kennedy, John F. 39
Kennerley, Kerri-Anne 161
Ketchell, Daniel 130
Key, John 118
Koch, David 130
Krall, Diana 59
Kroger, Michael 31

L
Langer, Justin 83
Lee, Spike 116
LeFrak, Francine 74
LeFrak, Samuel J. 74
Lennon, John 166
Leno, Jay 138

Levine, Phillip 37
Lew, Solomon 19, 45, 79
Lewis, Lennox 118
Lockheart, Joe 37
Lubner, Richard 13
Lutteral, David "Luttsy" 121

M
Mandela, Nelson 8,13-28, 41, 55
Mapp, Grahame 28-29, 43
Markson, Leon 10, 82
Maroney, Susie 41
May, Thersea 41
McCauliffe, Terry 55-56
McCarthney, Paul 166
McMahon, Sir William "Billy" and Lady Sonia 159
Meares, Jodie 14, 17
Menzies, Sir Robert 107
Midler, Bette 146
Mitchell, Neil 117
Morris, Cameron 99
Morris, Shariyah 99
Morrison, Scott 41
Moss, Carrie Ann 43-44
Mort, Chris 87
Murdoch, Lachlan 20, 80, 82
Murdoch, Rupert 79
Murray, Andrew 140
Murray, Les 145

N
Newman, Sam 161
Norman, Greg 44
Nureyey, Rudolph 146

O

O, Jackie 41, 164
Obama, Barack 55
O'Keefe Peter 55
Osibisa 151
Ovett, Steve 163

P

Pacino, Al 91-92
Packer, James 17-19, 68, 79
Packer, Kerry 18, 20
Peacock, Andrew 31
Pele 7, 142, 145-156
Penn, Mike 36
Phillips Jeremy 18
Pirro, Judge Jeanine 98-99
Pitt, Brad 58, 124
Placks, Elliot 21
Powell, Colin 59
Pratt, Anthony 68, 104, 107, 113
Pratt, Richard 20, 79

Q

Quaid, Dennis 33

R

Rania, Queen 59
Raptis, Jim 161
Reed, Tara 165
Rich, Jodee 20
Rivkin, Rene 158, 160
Robertson, John 31
Ross, Julia 42
Russo Sarina 51, 74, 80, 113-114

S

Schwarzenegger, Arnold 81, 103, 128-143, 168
Sharrouf, Khaled 125
Sheeran, Ed 170
Shriver, Sargent 138
Singleton, John 19, 87
Smith, Chris 150
Spacey, Kevin 58
Spears, Britney 70
Steenburgen, Mary 58
Stefanovic, Karl 130
Stevenson, Adlai 35
Streisand, Barbra 57, 59
Stroumboulopoulos, George 168
Sutcliffe, Ken 150
Swerner, Kane 151-152, 154-156
Symond, John 42

T

Taylor, James 166
Thatcher, Maggie 107
Trump, Donald 41, 82, 129
Trump, Melania 82
Tua, David 118
Turnbull, Malcom 67, 107
Turner, Ted 59
Twain, Mark 76
Tyson, Kiki 119-120, 127
Tyson, Mike 115-128, 142
Tyson, Milan 119, 128
Tyson, Morocco 119, 128

U

U2 58

V
Van Damme, Jean-Claude 125

W
Walker, Don 93
Walker, John 162
Warhol, Andy 165
Warne, Shane 14
Waterman, Denis 151
Webber, Andrew Lloyd 146
Weiss, Gary 19
Welch, Racquel 157-162
West, Kanye 97
Whitlam, Gough 22
Whyte, Robert 19
Wightman, Kip 121
Wilkins, Richard 130
Wilkinson, Lisa 130
Williams, Robin 58
Winfrey, Oprah 168-170
Worthington, Corey 165
Wran, Neville 62

Z
Zampatti, Carla 113

ABOUT THE AUTHOR

Max Markson is a Publicist, promoter, impresario and PR man. He has staged over 200 fundraising events giving over $40 million dollars to charity. Along the way he has been privileged to bring President Clinton on four tours to Australia and New Zealand and has hosted Nelson Mandela, President Bush Snr, New York Mayor Rudy Giuliani, Vice President Al Gore, Prime Minister Tony Blair, Kim Kardashian, Mike Tyson, Arnold Schwarzenegger, Pele and a host of others.